Your PhD Coach

Your PhD Coach

How to get the PhD experience you want

Jeff Gill and Will Medd

 Open University Press

Open University Press
McGraw-Hill Education
McGraw-Hill House
Shoppenhangers Road
Maidenhead
Berkshire
England
SL6 2QL

email: enquiries@openup.co.uk
world wide web: www.openup.co.uk

and Two Penn Plaza, New York, NY 10121–2289, USA

First published 2013

A catalogue record of this book is available from the British Library

ISBN–13: 978–0–33–524767–7 (pb)
ISBN–10: 0–33–524767–9 (pb)
eISBN: 978–0–33–524768–4

Library of Congress Cataloging-in-Publication Data
CIP data applied for

Typesetting and e-book compilations by
RefineCatch Limited, Bungay, Suffolk

Praise for this page

"Coaching empowered me to reclaim my PhD and this book will enable many more students to do the same. Will Medd and Jeff Gill have a deep understanding of the PhD process and students reading this book, at any stage in their PhD, will find themselves thinking "wow, that is exactly how I feel!". The book challenges the inevitability of the 'PhD steam-roller' and its comfortable and chatty tone creates a friendly guide for those struggling with the demands of a PhD and inspiration for those who want to get the most from the whole experience."

Beth Brockett, PhD Student, Lancaster Environment Centre,
Lancaster University, UK

"Medd and Gill go deep into the under the skin of what it is like to do a PhD, pull out the reality of the operation and offer some sound advice. They provide effective techniques to bust the 'gremlins' – the voices in the head - that can haunt postgraduate researchers and diminish the research experience. I urge all research students (and supervisors) to read this very accessible book. It will help them reflect deeper into their research experience and help build confidence in themselves and (re)gain satisfaction in their work and studies."

Dr Richard Hinchcliffe, Academic Development,
Centre for Lifelong Learning, University of Liverpool, UK

Contents

Acknowledgements   ix

Introduction   1

**Part I Setting firm foundations: say 'Yes!' to the
            perfect PhD day**   **7**

  1 Introduction to Part I and . . . how are you today?   9

  2 Throwing rocks before your PhD: learning
      to manage your inner critic   14

  3 What's the point of this path? Finding value in
      your perfect PhD   20

  4 Where is the pathway heading? Tapping into your
      bigger picture   29

  5 Bringing it all together: saying 'Yes' to the
      perfect PhD day   34

Part II Core themes in the PhD experience   **39**

  6 Out of control? In pursuit of better balance   41

  7 When self-doubt creeps in . . . how to find
      the superhero within   59

  8 Overwhelmed or underwhelmed? Finding enjoyment
      through your goals   74

  9 Stuck in a rut? Being creative   89

10 Distracted? Giving yourself permission to
   re-find your focus   105

11 On your own? Building better relationships   122

12 Too many knockbacks and brick walls? Building
   your PhD resilience   138

Part III Leadership in your PhD and beyond   **155**

13 The leader in you? Finding the authenticity to
   write your own story   157

References and further reading   165

Acknowledgements

Though we've worked together on and off for more years than we'd care to remember, this was our first joint writing project, and hopefully not our last! So we'd like to start by acknowledging each other and saying thank you, because that's the sort of thing coaches do!

We'd also like to acknowledge all the PhD coachees and workshop participants that we have worked with and whose experiences have informed this book – though none of the examples in the book relate to anybody specifically. Some have commented on drafts but in respect of the confidentiality of coaching will remain anonymous – thanks, you know who you are.

Other people have read and commented specifically on parts of the book or given us advice along the way, either telling us where we're going wrong or encouraging us to go further. So a big thanks to Rachel Medd, Rebecca Ellis, Jim Rose, Larry Wright, Dave Horton, Edith Graham, and Beccy Whittle. We want to thank Kathleen Cross for her meticulous, curious and sensitive corrections, suggestions and queries (we cannot recommend her enough as a proof reader and translator). Thanks also for the support from the publishers, in particular Shona Mullen, Katherine Hartle and Alexandra Nowosaid.

Finally, thanks to Tamsin for finding those elusive citations, and, of course, Bernard the Cat.

Introduction

Whether you are prospering, struggling or just mulling along, we have written this book to invite you to get a whole lot more from your PhD (and beyond) through techniques of self-coaching. This book is not just about surviving or even completing your PhD, it is about bringing vitality to the experience.

Why add to the long list of books on how to do a PhD? Don't they already map out what you need in order to complete a PhD successfully? There are plenty of books crammed full of details about what is required and how to go about it. They are important and we fully recommend that you read such books. At the same time, we want to suggest there is something more fundamental to engage with that underlies your ability to be at your best. That 'something' is the *experience* of doing a PhD. This book engages thoroughly with that experience and finding strategies for managing it in ways that help you thrive in, not just *survive*, your PhD.

Our aim is to bring a coaching philosophy to the PhD process. Timothy Gallwey, the 'grandfather' of coaching as we know it today, describes the 'inner game' of tennis in ways that seem just as pertinent to the PhD process:

> This is the game that takes place in the mind of the player, and it is played against such obstacles as lapses in concentration, nervousness, self-doubt and self-condemnation . . . it is played to overcome all habits of mind which inhibit excellence in performance.
>
> (1997: xix)

This is what coaching aims to address and why it is relevant to your PhD experience: the inner game of the PhD. It is about finding ways to transform the interferences that keep you from translating your wonderful potential into what you want to achieve in the PhD and beyond.

While people experience the PhD process in many different ways, there are also some common threads:

- *The PhD experience can be a struggle*: the pain of writing, general procrastination, insecurity and self-doubt, a sense of being over-whelmed by theory or data, pressure to finish, low motivation, a weighty feeling of dread pushing down on your shoulders, tricky relationships with supervisors, stage fright at the thought of presenting a conference paper, the struggle to balance the commitments of the PhD with the rest of life.
- *The PhD experience can be an adrenalin-inducing challenge*: how to keep alive the excitement of contributing to knowledge, how to drive the work onwards to get publications, where to take future research, how best to enhance your employability options within and beyond academia, how to engage with the wider research community, how to do the very best you can.
- *The PhD can be an awkward and contradictory combination of both*: finding writing painful and yet also wanting to push for publications; feeling stage fright while also wanting to engage with a wider community; sensing the excitement of contributing to knowledge alongside the weight of anxiety.

Of course, what you are experiencing will be unique to you: it is, after all, *your* experience! The question is, is that how you want it to be? For those who are experiencing the PhD as an emotional roller-coaster of insecurity, self-doubt and sheer dread, surely there must be a better way? For those who are getting on just fine and want to push for so much more, surely it is possible to engage in a process of personal development that involves learning from others? For those caught up between potentially exhausting tensions, surely there is a way to make that experience a productive and more fulfilling one? We think the answer to each of these questions is yes. Our hope with this book is to help you explore them for yourself.

Wherever you are right now – plagued by self-doubt, eager to get on, caught in a state of tension or simply curious – we've written this book because we've learnt from our combined experiences of doing a PhD, supervising PhDs, PhD coaching and running PhD workshops that the PhD experience can be what *you* choose to make it. It does not have to be how it is. Engaging with some coaching philosophy and with some added tips and tricks, we offer ways through which can make all the difference to your PhD experience (and beyond). You can change your experience of writing, of supervision, of procrastination, of motivation, of data collection and of all the other elements that go to make up the PhD experience for you. And (this is the best bit) you can enjoy it all at the same time!

At this point we imagine you have many doubts about how much you can change your PhD experience. This would hardly be surprising because there are a whole set of factors influencing your experience which may be outside your control: the limits of the university or your department; disinterested or over-interested supervisors; a wealth of literature, data, theories you need to sift through; a host of extraneous demands beyond the PhD process; and so on. Will remembers all too well feeling lost and emotionally drained during the middle stages of his PhD. He also remembers the answer one otherwise supportive supervisor gave him when he asked for advice: 'I went through that, that's just how it is with a PhD. Everyone experiences it, it's part of what you have to go through.' There was no other way, it seemed. This was, and remains, a common story. It is almost as if doing a PhD involves some sort of rite of passage in which such experiences have become inevitable.

Of course, there are some things which are beyond your capacity to change. However, the questions we raise are: How do you want to respond to all that? How much do you want to allow all those burdens to impact on your experience? On your emotions, your goals, your drive, your ambitions? How much power do you want those factors to exert over you and your sense of who you are in the world?

One sure way of making those factors extremely powerful is to turn them into your own internal voice. We all do it for much of the time. In fact, you might be doing it right now (if not, by the way, great – don't force it!). Later on in the book we're going to introduce a character which for now we'll call *the Gremlin* (others might prefer to call it the saboteur, the persecutor, the interrupter, the pressurizer, the demon, the bully, the inner critic, or some such name). Everyone has their own Gremlin figure. Put simply, following Rick Carson in *Taming Your Gremlin*, 'the gremlin is the narrator in your head' (2003: 3). It is a narrator that tends to be particularly good at putting us under pressure, limiting our possibilities and generally making us feel bad. It makes up sentences that include words and phrases such as: 'should do'; 'should have'; 'ought to'; 'ought to have'; 'must do'; 'had to'; 'but'; 'what if'; 'if only'; 'be careful'; 'don't risk it'; 'you have no choice'; 'you're not good enough'; 'you can't'. . . Your Gremlin voice may be telling you already all the reasons why your PhD experience is like it is, why it has to be so, and why it is going to be impossible to make any changes. 'That's just the way it is with a PhD.' If this is the case, just notice that voice for the moment, respectfully acknowledge its existence, and try and allow yourself to carry on reading nonetheless (perhaps even if just to prove yourself right, something Gremlins love!).

The bottom line of our message is, it all comes down to a shift in perspective. You do not have to accept 'that's just the way it is'. Will couldn't accept his supervisor's perspective and that is where the origins of this book began. We'll set them out briefly, as this helps to explain the ethos of the book. We met some years before Will's PhD, both of us working in the outdoor industry. Jeff had become particularly interested in the psychology of learning and coaching, and Will had become interested in the psychology of competition and how to be 'in the zone'. Some years later, Jeff had become an NLP (neuro-linguistic programming) coach and Will was struggling with his PhD and was very much out of the zone. Will explained to Jeff how everyone seemed to experience their PhD in this way and he bemoaned the inability of academics to respond in helpful ways. As a bit of an experiment, Jeff offered to try some coaching with Will, whose problems centred particularly on how to write about a difficult piece of theory. Jeff got Will doing some quite odd stuff for a budding academic: standing in different places; wearing different hats; moving back and forth along a timeline; visualizing his writing in different colours; thinking like an alien; reframing sticky problems into exciting and productive opportunities, and suchlike. It worked. Will found a way to shift into a different mood to approach his PhD, separating his sense of self-worth from the writing itself. He found his flow and drafted the next two chapters of his thesis more fluidly, receiving highly positive feedback from his supervisors. Better still, he started to enjoy it. He completed his PhD, went on to support friends in completing theirs and, as a lecturer later on, became interested in developing coaching skills to enhance the PhD process as a supervisor and PhD coach. Which is where we both joined forces again, running workshops, coaching PhD students, and capturing in this book some of what we have learnt in the process.

A shift in perspective made all the difference; nothing else had changed. The theory was still difficult. Other people were still much better at theory than Will. Yet Will could still make his contribution and could feel good about himself.

The argument we are proposing here runs deep. It is captured particularly powerfully by Victor Frankl in his book, *Man's Search for Meaning*. Frankl was an Austrian psychiatrist, neurologist and Holocaust survivor, who stated that 'everything can be taken from a man [or woman] but one thing: the last of the human freedoms – to choose one's attitude in any given set of circumstances, to choose one's own way' (1963: 104). Our aim here is not to get into a debate about existential philosophy and the 'will to meaning'. Instead, we want to draw attention to a key foundation of our approach, namely, that *you have the ability to choose* the attitude, the perspective, from which to approach and find meaning in your PhD experience. The challenge is to find the perspective, or indeed perspectives, that work for you in making the PhD experience what you want it to be.

So how does it work?

Our view is that whatever the particular area of your PhD experience you are concerned with, there are some fundamental principles or foundations that come into play. These are set out in the short chapters that form Part I of the book. Part I needs to be engaged with before you address the chapters in Part II. Part II is based on core themes that arise for people during the PhD experience, namely, balance, confidence, motivation, creativity, focus, relationships, resilience and authenticity. Part III is about leadership in your PhD.

These foundations and the core themes relate to all the aspects of the PhD. That is why we do not have specific chapters on particular areas of the PhD. Through our coaching work we have found that issues of balance, confidence, motivation, creativity, focus, relationships, resilience, authenticity apply in different ways at different times and in different combinations to all areas of the PhD, including writing, supervision, fieldwork, analysis, career development, the viva, etc.

As a self-coach guide, this book is not designed to be just read. Coaching is very much about learning through 'doing'. We have deliberately made the book conversational to help you find out what works for you in being with your PhD. Our assumption, expectation and request are that you will be creative, curious and active in your engagement with this book. To aid you, each chapter offers some questions, some challenges, some vignettes and a checklist. The questions are aimed to provoke some reflection about what is really at stake for you. The challenges invite you to engage in activities in ways that are relevant for you. The vignettes illustrate how the ideas we are offering have worked for other people. While they are based on real experiences that have cropped up in our coaching, for obvious reasons, the names and exact details are fictitious. The checklists at the end of Part I and the end of each chapter in Part II are there to provoke you to find ways of being responsible and accountable to the actions you want to take to experience the change you are looking for.

Before you jump in though, it is time to turn the focus on you! Core to the power of coaching are the questions that are being asked. To get the most out of this book and the self-coaching techniques we are offering, you need to get into the habit of asking yourself new questions. So some questions we have for you are:

- What is it about your current situation that has made you pick up this book?
- What do you hope to change by reading this book and how will you know if reading this book has made a difference to your PhD experience?
- How do you want to approach this book? From a place of curiosity, practicality, critique, experiment, for a bit of fun?
- When is the best time for you to read chapters in this book? Where will you be?

How you answer these questions – that is, the perspective you take in reading this book – might make all the difference to what you get out of it . . .

Part I

Setting firm foundations
Say 'Yes!' to the perfect PhD day

1

Introduction to Part I and . . . how are you today?

The pathway is smooth, why throw rocks before you?
(Chinese proverb)

What would having a perfect day mean for you?

How does your attitude affect the kind of day you experience?

What do you want each day to say about you?

Imagine the perfect PhD day. How would the day start? What would you be working on? What would you be achieving? Would you be with people? Would you be alone? Where would you be – in a library, in your office, in a café, at home, in the field? What would be around you – computer, desk, comfy chair, books, coffee, radio? What else might the day involve that isn't directly 'the PhD'? Perhaps some sport, fresh air, coffee with colleagues, a seminar, an art gallery, some music? What about the end of the day? How would work finish? What would happen next? Who would you be with? Where would you be?

Wouldn't it be amazing if we could create the perfect PhD day, every day, day after day throughout the PhD? Such days would look different for each of us. We each have different visions of our lives within which the PhD plays a part, we have different values that we want the PhD to fulfil, and we have different ambitions for the PhD itself. People are also at different stages and have different kinds of PhD work to do. So each person's perfect PhD day will look quite different and will change over time. But can our PhD days ever be perfect? All sorts of events happen, all the time. Life, as well as the specific world of the PhD, can rarely happen just as you've planned it, however hard you try.

Indeed, isn't that why people describe doing a PhD as being on a roller-coaster? One minute you're on top of the world, with such clarity and aspiration: you got the funding, your panel gave you fantastic feedback, your conference paper has been accepted, fieldwork was really exciting, your analysis has found something new . . . and the next, it's crashing down at ever increasing speed: you're getting nowhere and can't see the end of it, you had some difficult feedback from your supervisor or they didn't even read your work, the theory is too hard to understand, someone else has said it already, 'What's the point?' Things happen during the PhD that you really can't control, and sometimes that's tough, really tough.

What, then, if the perfect PhD day was not determined by the world 'out there' and instead was about the world 'in here'? What if the perfect day was about how you approached the day, whatever happened? Could the perfect PhD day be possible in a different sort of a way? A way in which fulfilment comes from responding to events in ways we value, rather than from the events being exactly how we think they should be? A day in which, to paraphrase Victor Frankl cited in the Introduction, you 'choose [your] attitude in any given set of circumstances, [you] choose [your] own way' (1963: 104). Could it be that there is a smoother pathway on which to experience the PhD, and we just need to stop throwing rocks before us?

Part I then is about how to create a smoother pathway for the PhD experience, how to make each day the perfect PhD day, whatever happens. Here's how:

- Noticing just how you are, really are, as you start your day – (this chapter).
- Finding ways to manage your inner critic (the Gremlin, saboteur, etc.) who stops you, pushes you, and generally throws rocks before you on the PhD path – (Chapter 2).

- Reminding yourself what you really value about doing a PhD (after all, you could quit right now!) and how the pathway can be smooth – (Chapter 3).
- Capturing the bigger picture of the PhD and beyond (and where that pathway might be heading) – (Chapter 4).
- Saying 'yes' to the day ahead – (Chapter 5).

How are you today?

How are you today? Now if we had met in the street or the university corridor and we'd asked that, you'd probably assume it was a matter of common courtesy. Your answer would most likely be one of common courtesy too. 'I'm fine, thank you, and you?' Or perhaps, 'Really good, how are you?' Or 'Not too bad, how about you?'

This book is not about courtesy; we really are asking you, how are you? Or rather, we want you to ask yourself 'How am I today?' We want to suggest you spend a few moments noticing, being as honest as you can with yourself, and acknowledging whatever you find. Each day brings different moods, different states or feelings. We may start the day tired, anxious, excited, pessimistic, optimistic, sad, happy, hot, cold, a complex bundle of all sorts of things. We never know what we'll wake up with. Yet surely it is so important to acknowledge how we are when we think ahead to what we can expect for the day.

Challenge: Noticing how you are

The first challenge is simply to notice how you are:

- First of all, note how are you in your body? What sensations are you experiencing? Sore, hot, cold, strong, weak, achy, alive, twitchy, tense, relaxed, sleepy, stimulated, restless, heavy, light?
- Then, emotionally, how are you feeling? Are you happy, sad, angry, excited, hurt, guilt-ridden, anxious, expectant? Again, jot down some notes.
- And finally, how's your outlook? Pessimistic, optimistic, nonplussed?

At this point, simply notice, acknowledge and be aware of how you are today, how you really are. Perhaps in that noticing you may start to see some links between how you are in your body, how you are feeling, and your general outlook for the day. Note: some people find it helpful to keep a note of how they are over a period of time, as a sort of mood map, to see if any patterns emerge. For the moment though, we want you to focus on . . . well, this moment!

Given how you are in this moment, what is realistic for you to achieve today?

Always too tired . . .?

Gina had a young baby who wasn't settling well at night. Needless to say, despite her and her partner's best efforts to encourage the baby to sleep, nothing was working. So Gina's PhD days often started with a sense of being shattered before she'd got anywhere near her work. Gina was becoming so demoralized. She had been setting daily goals based on a way of working she'd developed before she'd had a baby. Needless to say, the goals were impossible to achieve and so Gina carried a constant sense of failure. After some reflection Gina realized she was constantly setting herself up for failure. Gina realized that, in the context of her young baby, she couldn't realistically give her all to her PhD in the way she used to work. Her priorities had changed and she needed to find another way. Gina developed a different strategy. She developed her own 'energy gauge' to test each morning when she got to her desk. According to the gauge, she'd adjust the goals for what she needed to do on her PhD accordingly. Some days were, say, 50 per cent energy, in which case she assessed the ideal goals she'd set if she had 100 per cent energy, and worked out a 50 per cent version instead. Gina found herself feeling better towards the end of each day because she started to achieve what had become more realistic goals for herself. Interestingly, now she had also stopped 'worrying' about being tired, she found that she had more energy to focus on work instead of worrying about what she wasn't doing, and started to achieve much more than she would have expected, even when she was tired.

Summary

The question we have raised is so simple and yet huge, so worthy of a pause. Coaching is about looking forwards. To look forwards, you need to know where you are. That includes where you are emotionally. So that is our starting point to the perfect PhD day: to ask yourself how you are and look forward from there.

2

Throwing rocks before your PhD

Learning to manage your inner critic

Knowing how we are is one thing – it's quite another when we start to get cross or frustrated because of how we think we 'ought' to be. This chapter is about that voice in our heads, that internal narrator, the inner critic, which interrupts what we are doing and somehow says you need to be doing things differently (or even not at all!). Different authors have referred to versions of it in different ways, including the 'Inner Critic' (Greene 2008), the Gremlin (Carson 2003), Self 1 (Gallwey 1997), the Saboteur (Kimsey-House et al. 2011). Other words PhD students have come up with include the persecutor, the interrupter, the pressurizer, the demon, the bully . . . The point is, it comes in all sorts of shapes, sizes and forms. And there are times while doing a PhD when it can be particularly persistent, loud and irritating. It often jumps out at you just when you thought things were going well, raising all kinds of self-doubt, sometimes trying to stop you ('what's the point?'), sometimes trying to push you harder ('you're not fast enough') and always unhelpful! Always throwing rocks before you!

Although it comes in all sorts of shapes and forms, there are some great ways to spot it. First, it likes to use some very particular words like: 'should do', 'should have', 'ought to', 'ought to have', 'must do', 'must have', 'have to', 'but', 'what if?', 'if only', 'be careful', 'don't risk it', 'there is no choice', 'you're not good enough', 'you can't', 'it's not possible' . . . Second, what it tends to say often leaves you feeling disempowered and without many choices. It tells you what the situation is and why you either 'must' do X or 'can't' do Y. And third, which is where it really digs its heels in, it likes to raise the stakes so that everything matters (if you 'don't' or 'can't' or 'won't', then everything is over!).

Before we go any further, please note this. Your Gremlins (we've decided to use that word from now on) are not real people. When they've started to think about their Gremlins, we've heard PhD students say things like, 'Oh, I know my Gremlin alright, it's my supervisor' or, 'Oh, crikey, that's my mum that says those things'. Here's the deal: it might be that 'real' people reinforce your Gremlin voice BUT BUT BUT the internal Gremlin is your own creation, it is your own inner voice. It might be a voice you learnt from somebody else, but it's you and you alone that keeps it alive. In a way, then, it's a figment of your imagination. It does not belong with anyone else and, as we'll see, it can be under your management.

So how can we tackle our Gremlins? How can we disempower them? You probably know your Gremlins quite well already even if you've not actually met face to face. They are a master of disguise and can be oh so powerful in the PhD process unless, quite simply, you notice them.

Challenge: Getting to know your Gremlins

- First of all, notice your Gremlins. Look out over the next few days when your inner voice is using Gremlin-type words ('ought', 'should', 'shouldn't', 'must', 'must not', 'can't'). For example, 'you don't know enough about that topic', 'you ought to have done more reading', 'you shouldn't risk writing anything wrong', 'you're not analysing hard enough', 'don't make the wrong choice about the data'. Note how it tends to generalize. Look out for when that inner voice is raising the stakes to be all or nothing: 'get this wrong and the PhD is over', 'it's all too much, I can't do it any more', 'my field-work is a disaster', 'don't make a mistake here', 'change is too scary, be careful'.

- Next, name your Gremlins. Some people call them 'John' or 'Harry', others name them to capture what they are saying, 'Hedge your bets', 'Mr Risk Averse', others use cartoon characters or characters from novels – whatever works for you so that you have a shorthand. Some people like to get creative with their Gremlins. What does it look like? You might even draw a picture of them.
- Then, identify the consequence of your Gremlins. Simply complete the following sentence: My Gremlin is called. . . . . He or she is very fond of saying. . . . . . The consequence is that I. . . . . .

Some PhD Gremlins' statements we've come across

'Doubting Thomas' is very fond of saying 'I doubt you'll be good enough for that theory.' The consequence is I don't engage with the debate that really matters to my PhD and I retreat from saying what I really want to; instead I muddle through dissatisfied.

'Hedge your bets' is very fond of saying 'Don't risk losing out, you should keep your options open.' The consequence is I don't commit and when things get tricky with my writing, I tend to start thinking of other options or things I could be doing instead of working through it.

'All or nothing' likes to say 'You must get this right because everything depends on it.' The consequence is I tend to feel anxious and hold back for fear of failure and my fieldwork is going really slowly.

'Control freak' tends to say 'You should make sure it's all planned out before you do anything at all.' The consequence is I spend time mapping everything out and avoiding doing what's in front of me and often re-planning, writing more 'to do' lists, just to make sure.

'Urgent' tends to say 'You must clear all this stuff before you start on that.' The consequence is I spend time on loads of little tasks and avoid doing the big stuff like writing.

So you've spotted and named your Gremlins, and spotted what they do for you. Noticing your Gremlins and spotting the consequences are half-way there to ultimately managing them. It's almost as if, by noticing the Gremlins, they start to lose their power. You'll probably find over time that more appear, so keep this as an open challenge and see what else emerges.

You're not good enough

Vicky was an interdisciplinary research student who felt really insecure about her knowledge of the disciplines she was working within. She didn't feel confident to write about the different areas ('but I might get it wrong'), she didn't feel able to ask questions with her peers ('mustn't risk looking stupid') and she was sure her supervisors had their doubts ('they don't think I am good enough'). She felt under so much pressure to know everything in each discipline ('I should, must work harder') and was ready to give up. She felt there was no way out. Once Vicky started to notice her Gremlins and what it felt like to listen to them, something started to shift. She saw how powerful they had become, and yet they had no evidence to back up their story. Quite the opposite: she had passed her confirmation panel with flying colours, she had been asked to present her work at workshops, and in fact, though she didn't know it, her supervisors described her as one of their most interesting students. In fact, Vicky turned this completely around and realized her strength was the questions she asked because of the insight from working across different disciplines. This became her source of excitement and motivation.

Before you move on, you have some options here. One might be to stay with what you know – after all, you've had these Gremlins for some time and you're doing a PhD, so that's pretty good going. So why bother to get rid of the Gremlins now? We want to strike a deal with you. Bear with us for this next exercise and the rest of this chapter, and if you find it is all too much, you can, of course, opt into having your Gremlins back. One of the nice things about Gremlins is that they are very loyal; however harshly you treat them, they are always willing to come back to be with you! For now, though, let's see what you can do to manage them.

Challenge: Learning to manage your Gremlins

- *Daily Gremlin spotting.* This is a simple task and you can be as creative with it as you like and elaborate on it in a way that works for you. Use ten pages, with all your Gremlins printed out, one on each page. Whenever you spot a Gremlin, cross it off the list and throw that page in the bin. You have ten pages. See if you can spot all ten in one day. Or over the week.

Every now and then the Gremlin really digs in its heels. It's worth checking something here. Is there some truth you need to acknowledge? Is there something the Gremlin is saying that you need to listen to? There might be, and as you work through the book that will become clearer. However, sometimes it's simply a bad habit of listening to the Gremlin and it won't let go:

- *Disempowering Gremlins.* Again, lots of options here. Some will work for you and some won't, so this is a menu of choices and no doubt there are more you can create. Imagine your Gremlin as vividly as possible.
  - What colour is your Gremlin? Try changing it to something else. Try different colours until it feels different. Try different patterns over it: perhaps something stripy, something ridiculous?
  - How loud is the Gremlin? Change the volume, does that help? Change the tone, what happens? A squeaky voice perhaps?
  - How big is the Gremlin? Change the size, what happens?
  - How close to you is the Gremlin? What happens if it moves further and further away, until it's smaller and smaller . . .?
  - Keep trying different things that change its form in a way that, for you, disempowers it.

Impossible to move forwards

Pete was near the end of his PhD, which he'd really enjoyed, and had come for some coaching about next steps after his PhD. He was interested in post-doc research, in going for lectureships, or working in the commercial world and even setting himself up as a consultant. Lots of options. After a couple of coaching sessions it was clear there were many Gremlins at work. It was impossible for Pete to move forward because of the 'what ifs' and the 'shoulds' and the 'can't because' and the 'it's either that or that and nothing else'. And they weren't shifting. After confronting Pete about his Gremlins' power, he admitted that he hadn't been doing any work with them in-between coaching sessions. He couldn't see the point of the exercises. After the coach challenged him to take it more seriously, he was amazed at what happened next. He built on the idea of Gremlin spotting with a graph (he was a scientist). Not only did he then see for himself just how powerful they were, he realized that following the exercises also took away some of the Gremlin's power. Over the next few weeks Pete gained much more clarity about the options and choices for the way forward, and in particular, that some of the things he wanted to do could be combined and required similar actions from him at this point in time.

Summary

The second part of smoothing out your pathway to the perfect PhD day is done, learning to manage your Gremlins. It'll take time to get more skilled at this, and of course the more skilled you are, the more skilled those Gremlins may get. So it's important to keep working on this. When faced with a decision (not) to do something you can now double-check: how loud is my Gremlin here? What self-limiting assumptions am I imposing? What is really at stake?

3

What's the point of this path?

Finding value in your perfect PhD

There are only two tragedies in life: one is not getting what one
wants, and the other is getting it.

(Oscar Wilde, *Lady Windermere's
Fan*, Act 3)

Imagine if each morning began with a moment of reflection on what
it is you value about the day ahead. It can be so easy to forget what it
was about the pathway you are on that was particularly important
to you at the time you set out on it. When caught in the quagmire
of the PhD – whether it's the labour of writing, the monotony of
fieldwork or analysis, the sense of little income, exasperation with
your supervisors or struggles with balancing the rest of life – we can
forget just what it is that matters to us about doing, and achieving,
the PhD as well as other daily things we do. Part of creating the perfect
day is about aligning what we are doing with what we hold dear, what
we value.

It is so easy to overlook and take for granted what is really important
to us. From our coaching point of view we want to help you get the most
out of each day of your PhD, to help you create your perfect day: values

are about what we stand for, what motivates us, and what makes us who we are. What could be more perfect than to honour our values each and every day during our PhD?

By values, we mean those things that, when you honour them, make you feel good about yourself, make you feel fulfilled and congruent. At some point in the not too distant past something brought you to want to do a PhD. Perhaps you were motivated by an idea or specific problem that you wanted to pursue further. Perhaps that was for its own sake, a matter of simple curiosity, or perhaps it was because you wanted to contribute to pushing the boundaries of knowledge. Perhaps you were motivated to do the PhD to pursue a profession, perhaps as an academic or industry researcher. Perhaps the PhD was a way to engage in or address an issue you wanted to change, a motivation to change the world, the environment or society in some way. Or perhaps the PhD was a bit of respite, a chance to not yet decide on what do to. A chance to extend student life? A chance to reflect on life and what it offers you? Perhaps it was pride and prestige – you want to be a 'Dr'? Or even pressure – you did well and felt obliged when a professor offered you funding . . . And (*and* not *or*!), it was some sort of combination of parts of all these things? And other things too? And indeed perhaps it was something you no longer hold onto, that you no longer value?

A slight detour here to consider the possibility you want to quit your PhD. There is many a time when people want to quit their PhD. Sometimes this may be Gremlin talk: you ought to be doing something else, you're not good enough at this, you should this, that, or the other. It may not be Gremlins: it may be that you've learnt something about yourself and what matters to you, and that means you want to make a positive decision to stop doing a PhD. Stopping is an option. You could. Have some Gremlins just emerged for you? 'But that isn't an option, it is not possible because. . . .' There may be all sorts of reasons, justifications and pressures as to why stopping isn't an option. And yet, however hard this seems, it really is still an option, a very real option. The flip side of this is also tough at first: you can take responsibility for choosing to do your PhD. You can no longer blame the world out there for making you feel miserable, you could leave. Enough of this fierceness! We can turn this into something altogether more upbeat. For those who find you are ready to leave – and it may well be that the following exercises reinforce this decision – well done for making a brave decision! The question we now invite you to ask is, what are you saying 'yes' to?

What values does that decision honour for you? And for those who are continuing with the PhD, exactly the same! Well done for making a brave decision! The question we invite *you* to ask is, what are you now saying 'yes' to? What values does continuing with your PhD fulfil for you?

The power of 'I have a right to . . .'

Christian was feeling completely trapped, was sleeping badly and had no motivation. He hated the situation he was in. He had convinced himself that he didn't like reading academic work, found writing a complete bore, couldn't stand the play of intellectual discussion at conferences, found the university stale and, all in all, felt the grass was greener elsewhere. If only he could work out just what that elsewhere was!

Christian stood back a little and, first of all, put aside some of his Gremlins: he knew he didn't want to make his decisions based on their input. Yet something was niggling him. He dug a little deeper to explore a particularly powerful Gremlin that was saying 'You should be doing something else.' To lift the weight of that voice, he changed it to 'You *could* be doing something else.' Even that reframing – a tool we'll come back to from time to time – shifted something for Christian. It created a world of possibility – 'could' – rather than a world of entrapment – 'should'. Taking that a stage further, and lifting the pressure off even more, he added the idea that, in fact, not only could he leave the PhD and find something else, he had every right to. Christian created a little mantra for himself that he said each morning: 'I have the right to leave my PhD', 'I have the right to find something else to do', 'I have the right to honour my values' and 'I have the right to find each day fulfilling'. Realizing the power of his 'right to' created a world of opportunities for him, including – and this is the twist – the right to carry on his PhD! Which is exactly what he did because, having lifted the burden of 'I should', that opened up the possibilities of 'I could', and having then explored what he really valued (rather than the voice of the Gremlin), he discovered that, with the right balance of other things in his life, the PhD was exactly what he wanted to be doing. And he had a right to carry on with it: 'I have a right to do the PhD', 'I have a right to enjoy the PhD', 'I have a right to do what matters to me'.

Challenge: Identifying the things that matter to you, your values

Whether you are on the edge of stopping, stuck in a rut, looking for more motivation, wanting to push your experience further or just simply curious, a bit of a values check will probably help you out. How are you doing with your values? How clear are you on what you value in life? And how clear are you as to how the PhD process fulfils those values? That's the focus here: to get more in touch with your values and start to align your PhD experience to the things that matter, that really matter, to you.

The following exercises will help you identify and work with your values. We recommend you do them all, perhaps over a period of time, and repeat them from time to time to see what else emerges.

- *Peak experience*: Spend 15 minutes holding in your mind a specific time when things were just so, as follows. In a comfortable place, take some deep breaths and start to remember a moment, a specific moment when everything for you was just right. It might be in the recent past, or it might be some years ago. In coaching sessions PhD students have used all sorts of 'peak' experiences. Sometimes people identify a particular moment when they passed an exam. Or a time when they felt really on top of their sport. Others choose an example from a previous job when they felt they were really in the flow. The peak experience doesn't have to be from the PhD experience. The important thing is to choose one that works for you. It's about a moment when you felt good and on a roll; ignore whatever happened next. Try and remember that moment in as much detail as possible. Bring it alive: where were you? Who were you with? How were you feeling? What colours come to mind? What could you hear? What were you doing? What sensations did you feel in your body? What would somebody watching you have seen? Now, keeping it alive, start to jot down the things that really mattered to you in that moment. What made everything just so? What was it that made everything feel just right? What was really important to you in that moment? Write down key words that describe what really mattered to you in this moment.

This is work in progress – sit with those words for the day, add to them, adjust them, elaborate them. You can use the template given here to help.

My Peak Experience

My peak experience was

....

At the time I felt

....

The values I was honouring were

....

Now we suggest you do the opposite:

* *Trough experience*: Spend 15 minutes holding in your mind a specific time when things were just not so! You might decide to do this on a different day. Like the last task, take some deep breaths. Now, think of a moment, a specific moment when you felt angry, frustrated, annoyed or really quite upset. It might be in the recent past, or it might be some years ago. It might be something someone said or something someone did, something you heard about, something that wound you up. It can be specific to the PhD or something entirely different. The important thing is to choose a moment that you can remember vividly. Try and remember that moment in as much detail as possible. Bring it alive: where were you? Who were you with? How were you feeling? What colours come to mind? What could you hear? What were you doing? What sensations did you feel in your body? What would somebody watching you have seen? Now, keeping it alive, jot down the things that really affected you in that moment. What made you so angry, frustrated, annoyed or upset? What was really important to you that was being violated in that moment? Write down key words that capture this.

Again, you're building up more words that describe what really matters to you. Keep with the words through the day, build on them, develop them, add to them.

My frustrated, angry, annoyed, upset moment was

My frustrated, angry, annoyed, upset moment was

....

At the time I felt

....

The values that were being challenged, suppressed or confronted were

....

With the last two exercises you're building up a sense of key things that matter to you, and building up lists of words or phrases that capture those things, i.e., your values.

Challenge: Pulling together what matters to you

You've now got somewhere towards getting in touch with and becoming clearer about your values. You have two lists of key words. They probably overlap. And some may even be contradictory. Let's see. Let's bring together the different words that describe values. You can elaborate these at any moment you want.

- *Clustering your values.* Get a blank piece of paper and start to 'cluster' the words that go together to capture your different values. Give a name to each cluster to capture the essence of those values for you.

Some words that can capture our values . . .

Harmony	Solitude	Sustainability
Accomplishment	Resilience	Trust
Peace	Community	Elegance
Independence	Fun	Connection
Cooperation	Love	Risk taking
Aesthetics	Family	Joy
Growth	Fortitude	Beauty

Understanding	Kindness	Style
Empathy	Acknowledgement	Order
Recognition	Vitality	Being on the edge
Honesty	Prosperity	Dynamism
Tradition	Freedom to choose	Presence
Being understood	Spirituality	Authenticity
Supporting	Empowerment	Good speech
Integrity	Achievement	The outdoors
Nurturing	Excellence	Commitment

Note it is totally fine to have values that may appear contradictory. You may have a set of values about solitude and time for reflection, and a set of values about socializing and community. The good news is: you can have both. Perhaps not at the same time, but over time you can find the right balance (more on that in another chapter).

Hopefully, then, you've come up with a list of around seven to ten core values. You might find over time that you want to develop this list. You might realize that something isn't quite right. Feel free to add and make changes: it all helps in getting to know what really matters to you that much better.

- *Which values are the most important?* Now, using that list of core values, rank them. Based on how you feel today, how would you rank them in terms of importance to you? Don't worry: you can change the ranking, there is no right answer. And we're not forcing you to let go of any. Simply rank them: which is the most important, which the least? To help, try this for a bit of fun. You are in a hot air balloon. Some of that hot air is coming from your values and you are rising too fast and running out of oxygen. You need to come down a bit, you have to throw out two of your values. Which would you let go of? Which would you keep?
- *Are you living your values?* Next, give each of your values a score between 1 and 10. A score of 1 means you are hardly living (honouring) that value at the moment during your PhD experience, and a value of 10 means that you are fully living that value during your PhD experience.

The Value, Ranking, Score grid will help.

Value, Ranking, Score

Value	Ranking	Current Score
e.g. Having fun	3	4/10
e.g. Making a contribution	2	3/10
e.g. Solitude	6	5/10
Etc.	Etc.	Etc.

Challenge: One small step for values, one giant step for you!

You now have a list of values and a sense, indeed a ranking, of how much those values mean to you at this moment in time. And you have a sense, again a score, of the extent to which, during your PhD experience, you are honouring those values. Here's the challenge:

- *Honouring your values.* Identify one of the values that you would like to honour more. Think of what that value means to you. How could you approach the day ahead of you in a way that will improve that score? Don't put it off! Today, this day, what small step, however small, would take you towards improving that score for that value in your PhD experience? We dare you to give it a go . . . And note, by PhD experience we mean this in a holistic sense – it might be, for example, that booking yourself in for some kind of exercise would be part of improving the experience by honouring a value of health.

Make a big difference with a few small steps

Carmela was in the second year of her PhD and things were going pretty well, yet something wasn't feeling quite right. She was feeling a sense of dissatisfaction but couldn't put her finger on it. Carmela decided to explore what values she was honouring while doing her PhD. Her peak experience was a time during her Master's when she felt on top of her game, really engaged in the literature for an essay, and was also the departmental representative. She identified some key values around being at her best, being engaged, learning, making a contribution and working with others. When she turned to look at her PhD it became really clear that she was working really well, she was learning and she was engaged. What was missing, though, was a sense of making a contribution and working with others. She addressed this in few small steps: she put herself forward to co-organize some departmental seminars and to do some teaching. She also realized then that enabling others to learn became another important value in itself.

Summary

Fantastic! The third part of smoothing out the pathway towards the perfect PhD day is in place: 'honouring your values'. Over time, our understanding of our values can shift, we may add more words, gain more clarity, discover new values. When faced with a decision or a lack of motivation or when just feeling in the wrong mood, remind yourself which value you are honouring. Being aware of your values in this way will be a learning process.

4

Where is the pathway heading?

Tapping into your bigger picture

Our deepest fear is not that we are inadequate. Our deepest fear is that we are powerful beyond measure. It is our light, not our darkness, that most frightens us. We ask ourselves, who am I to be brilliant, gorgeous, talented, and fabulous? Actually, who are you not to be? Your playing small does not serve the world.

(Marianne Williamson, *A Return to Love: Reflections on the Principles of a Course in Miracles*. London: HarperCollins, 1992: 190–91)

Let's get back to the business of the pathway. It is so easy to get lost on the PhD pathway, so easy to forget why you're doing it, and so easy to lose sight of things that really matter to you. Here you are faced with a huge challenge, a challenge to undertake research that will make 'an original contribution' and to present that in 60,000+ words. It can feel like a painfully long and meticulous process with a very real possibility that only five people will ever read it from beginning to end (you, perhaps two supervisors (though not always) and two examiners (hopefully always!)). No wonder people sometimes feel it is pointless, find it a struggle to get motivated, and feel isolated or even withdrawn.

But isn't that such a narrow perspective? If you've followed what we've done so far, you'll have noticed just how you are today, you'll have stopped letting the Gremlins throw rocks before you, and you'll have smoothed out the pathway so that being on it is starting to honour your values. The great thing about being on the pathway is you can focus on each step without constantly worrying whether you are heading in the right direction. For that to be the case, though, since this pathway is a metaphor in which the precise direction is perhaps not always clear, it can be helpful to check in and reinvigorate ourselves with a sense of where it is we are heading in terms of the bigger picture.

Identifying your values feeds into that bigger picture. Here, though, we take a different tack, to further help place the PhD experience within a bigger sense of what you want your life to be about.

Another one of our detours here before we get to the next challenges for you. When we've run workshops with PhD students and talked about the bigger picture, someone always says, 'Yes, but what if the vision is unrealistic?' This is an important point – and one Gremlins love to raise whenever they get chance. And it's true: we have lots of what might seem to be apparently unrealistic visions (world peace, environmental harmony, justice). And perhaps, too, people have had such apparently unrealistic visions in the past: establishing women's voting rights, ending apartheid in South Africa, landing a person on the moon, personal computing, running a mile in less than four minutes, global communications networks, the end of the Cold War . . . The list continues. Remember Martin Luther King's 'I have a dream. . .'. There are three points we want to make here. The first is, why set your bigger picture small? What would you gain from that? How would it serve you? Why not hold onto something more powerful? How would that serve either you or the world at large? The second is, does it matter if that bigger picture turns out to be unrealistic? Does a child who fantasizes about becoming a World Cup footballer lose out by treasuring such a vision? Or does she gain from learning about fitness, skill development, dedication and team working? And third, which relates to the last point, the power of keeping hold of a bigger picture lies in how it translates into what we do now, how we conduct our everyday moments.

Challenge: What is the bigger picture for you?

In our experience, PhD students (and people generally!) relate to a sense of the bigger picture in different ways. These two exercises are based on your idea of your vision and what you see your purpose in life to be. You might find it helpful to come back to them; as learning takes place, your sense of the bigger picture will change.

- *My future*. Find somewhere special to you. Ideally, choose some-where that for you has a sense of space and feels inspiring. Perhaps a park, a favourite walk, a wood, a gallery, or whatever works best for you. You are more than your PhD, so when you do this let it encompass all of your life and extend beyond your PhD. In your special place, mark out the now (the time and date you are doing this) on the ground or floor, and then create a timeline that stretches out into the future. For example, if your special place is a park, the now might be represented by a particular park bench and your timeline might stretch out to a boating lake some distance away to represent the future. Next, slowly walk along your timeline, letting the weeks, months and years pass by until you reach a point several years ahead. Imagine at this point that you are experiencing the future you want and the one you often fantasize about. Consider the following questions about your future (not as things are right now) and jot down your answers: What have I got in this future that I really want? What am I doing with my life at this point in the future? How am I feeling? What have I achieved? Where am I? Who am I with? What am I like as a person? How do others describe me?

These are 'big' questions, so just go with it and jot down what comes into your head. This is work in progress.

- *My legacy*. Again, in a special place, begin at your starting point on a timeline and walk slowly along your timeline to the following four imaginary points in the future. Stop at each one and consider the following legacies:
  - What do you want your legacy to be when you finish your PhD and leave your university?
  - What do you want your legacy to be when you leave your next career, whatever that may be?
  - What do you want your legacy to be when you move on and leave your home or your community?
  - What do you want your legacy to be when you approach the later stages of life? What do you want people to say about you at your 80th birthday party? Or at your funeral?

Now sum up your thoughts about your legacy (or legacies) based on your answers to those questions. What does this tell you about your sense of a bigger picture?

- *Picturing my bigger picture.* Generate a picture of the bigger picture! Following either or both of the above exercises, and still in your special place, let an image pop into your mind that captures your bigger picture. This image doesn't have to mean anything to anyone else, it's just for you. Let your imagination run riot, anything goes here. If you are having trouble with this, just make something up and that will be just fine. Draw it or sketch it right there. A picture speaks a thousand words and thinking in pictures uses different intelligences and more creative parts of our brains. This is a neat way of summarizing and reminding yourself without the need for lots of words; it's like compressing a file on a computer. (And, by the way, perhaps there are other aspects of your PhD where some imagery, instead of words, might be helpful?)

Finally, to prompt you to think even more about your bigger picture, you could try this:

- *60 seconds to speak to the world.* Imagine you have 60 seconds on a stage and the whole world is listening. What would you say?
- *Texting the world.* If you had 30 words to text to everyone in the world, what would you say?

Beyond the PhD

Nick got into a bit of a pickle with his PhD and how to finish it. He was aiming to do a PhD by publication. All was going well, except that he had a conflict with his supervisor. Nick wanted to finish his PhD by publication as soon as possible, and the minimum requirement was four publications (which he had almost completed). His supervisor wanted more, however, because there were at least another two publications that he could develop from the data. For Nick, the issue was that he was ready to move on. He had a very clear sense of wanting to make a difference and be a mover and shaker in policy worlds. The PhD was important for the status of expertise it would give him in that world. Two more publications would add little, he felt, and would slow him down. The conflict was leading to a sticking point of what to do next.

Reflecting more on this bigger picture, Nick realized his sense of wanting to make change in the world was because he valued making a difference in the best way he could and to the best of his abilities. Taking this a step further, he realized it also meant making the most out of his PhD and that a couple of extra months finishing two more articles would mean he'd made the best of the results and made a more significant contribution to the research field. He also felt making a contribution to his relationship with his supervisor was important. Nick went on to develop two more chapters, and became a mover and shaker in the policy world, where continued links with his research group, following such a good relationship with his supervisor, led to a productive relationship of knowledge exchange that was key to his success.

Summary

Your bigger picture may not be fixed; you may feel it needs changing, tweaking, or that you want to start again. That is fine. Why shouldn't your sense of the bigger picture change as you learn more about yourself? What is useful, though, is that as you continue on the PhD journey, tapping into that sense of your bigger picture can help you stay on track. That can come in different forms. Sometimes it can be about reminding yourself of the importance of your PhD to that journey. And sometimes it can be about reminding yourself to keep the PhD in the right perspective.

5

Bringing it all together

Saying 'Yes' to the perfect PhD day

The problem with the PhD pathway is it shoots off in all sorts of directions and it isn't always clear if it's heading where we want it to. There are many twists and turns and, rather like a complex maze, we may take the wrong one. Do not fear, though: as Susan Jeffers points out in her (1987) book *Feel the Fear and Do It Anyway*, aircraft on autopilots are actually flying in the wrong direction 90 per cent of the time, yet they still arrive at their destination! Autopilots work on continually re-correcting for being off-course. So what we offer here is a way of pulling together what you've gained from the previous chapters in Part I to create your very own Satnav to guide you towards your perfect PhD day, every day!

The metaphor of a Satnav is quite handy here. When you switch your Satnav on each day it has to spend a bit of time orienting itself to where it is. It has to align itself to the orbiting satellites it can communicate with in order to plot your position. It then has to work out where you want to get to on your journey and map out the best route. And, of course, more advanced ones have a sort of radar, scanning for news of traffic problems or road blocks so that they can alter course as necessary. If you take a wrong turning or miss the junction, they will rapidly reassess the best option to keep you heading towards your destination. So too, then, with this PhD Satnav. It involves a daily calibration of how you feel, orbiting Gremlins, your values, your bigger picture and your destination for the day!

Another detour before we get to the final challenge: goal setting. We'll be setting out some strategies for goal setting for your PhD experience in another chapter. Here, though, it's useful to make a distinction between Goals and goals. In a way, Goals with a big 'G' is all of the above. It's about the Goal of your bigger vision, about how the things you will do in the day will honour your values, about how you are going to be in the day (see below). This is quite different from the goals you've set for your PhD (perhaps to finish a chapter, do x number of samples, interviews, etc., etc.). And it's quite different from the 'to do' list you might set yourself each day. The perfect PhD day, remember, is not about the world out there, it is about how you approach the day from within. It is about achieving the goal of how you want to be for the day, about choosing your attitude. The actions that follow from that will be the subject of future chapters.

Challenge: Saying yes to the perfect PhD day

There are many options, many choices facing us from the moment we get up each day. Sure, routine and habit often mean we do many things without thinking about it. When we do some things, and not others, we are saying 'yes' to them and 'no' to the others. These two words are immensely powerful. Think of your PhD and say 'no, no, no' a few times. How do you feel? Now think of your PhD and say 'yes, yes, yes' a few times. Notice any difference?

First thing in the morning, perhaps before you are at work, before you arrive in your office, or when at your desk, take a moment. Just five minutes is all you need, and it might make the world of difference to your day:

1   Notice how you are, emotions, sensations, outlooks – however weak or strong, just note them down, acknowledge they are present.
2   Note any Gremlins that seem to be lurking – you might find just one or two, or a few lined up waiting to interfere with your day (and maybe none, great!). Notice them, perhaps say 'Good morning!' or do any tricks that you have found help quieten them down for you.

3 Thinking about your day ahead, what values will you be honouring as you carry out your day? Remember these could be very specific to the task at hand (e.g., 'learning' from reading) and other values relevant to you at that time (e.g., 'family' or 'fitness'). Sometimes when faced with something you don't like doing but which is necessary, it can be useful to realize how doing it is all part of your wider values and your bigger picture.

4 Next tap into your bigger picture, remember what it is about and why it's important to you at this moment in time.

5 Now, given what you have in front of you for the day, and what values you are honouring, identify how you want to be during the day. That is, identify three ways of being you are saying 'yes' to in your day . . . the attitudes you want to bring to your perfect PhD day (see the diagram that follows for examples). Top tip here: if you are having trouble identifying saying 'yes' to things, try saying 'no' to three things first. And then switch them around. 'No to feeling anxious about my writing' might become 'Yes to being calm while I write'. Or 'No to the weight of my PhD on my shoulders' might become 'Yes to a sense of lightness and focus'. The box lists some common things we have found PhD students saying 'yes' to.

Ways of being you might say yes to

Ways of being you might say yes to . . .		
. . . to clarity	. . . to lightness	. . . to focus
. . . to being assertive	. . . to having fun	. . . to achieving my goals
. . . to being a good colleague	. . . to learning	. . . to adventure
. . . to security	. . . to engagement	. . . to excitement
. . . to calmness	. . . to honouring my values	. . . to commitment
. . . to health	. . . to resilience	. . . to caring
. . . to vitality	. . . to being alive	. . . to laughing
. . . to setting my agenda	. . . to love	. . . to being motivated

Yes to adventure

Anton was struggling with his data analysis. He was at a stage that involved some quite tricky lab work and he really didn't feel confident with it. It was dragging on, and though he was working hard, he wasn't achieving as much as he'd set out to each day. The problem was, Anton was putting off the difficult part each day and procrastinating with all sorts of other things, sometimes postponing the difficult bit for the next day, and so on. Motivation was low and each day had a heavy feel. Having tried to work out what was wrong and not really got anywhere, Anton worked on the exercises laid out in this chapter. He started each day remembering his bigger picture, putting down the Gremlins, and tapping into his values. He then also approached the challenge of the lab work by saying 'Yes to the challenge of something new', 'Yes to moving forwards each day', 'Yes to the adventure of the PhD'. The task itself was still just as hard, but Anton was now able to say 'Yes' to the task. Things started to move forward, and yes, it was hard . . . and worthwhile. Indeed, a few months on and Anton was teaching others in the lab the technique . . . while saying 'yes' to new challenges (including those around teaching!).

Finding what we want to say yes to can take practice. It can be particularly hard when we feel at the bottom of the trough. It can also be hard, *really* hard, to keep the feeling of 'saying yes' alive when things take a turn for the worse in the day or unexpected challenges jump out. Here are two ideas for bringing you back to a place where you are saying 'yes' to the perfect day:

- *Visualizing everything going well.* Just like high jumpers, skiers or racing drivers whom you see visualizing their 'success' before they perform, you can use a bit of mental rehearsal for the daily challenges of your PhD, i.e., imagining yourself doing something in just the way you want to do it. Imagine it going well. What are you feeling? What are you seeing? What are you hearing? What are you saying 'yes' to in that moment?
- *A constant reminder.* Sometimes, to really keep alive the spirit of saying 'yes', PhD students find it helpful to have a visual or audio cue. Sometimes a particular image comes up. Over time, PhD students have come up with all sorts of things that mean something specific to them: cartoon characters, pictures of fun fair rides, a particular

technology, yin and yang, dolphins, a bird, flower, rainbow, etc. What you can do is find a way to keep that image with you: create a picture, use it for a screen saver, a desktop, a badge, put it on the front of your diary, on your phone. Find somewhere that will be a constant reminder, a cue to saying 'yes' to how you want to be for the day. And the same goes for music and sounds.

Summary . . . and next steps

This is the last chapter in Part I – so 'Yes' to completing Part I perhaps? And 'yes' to refining your own way to create the perfect day: your own Satnav (or other metaphor if you've found one!). This is all very much a work in progress. There is no simple fix that will happen overnight. Keep building on the challenges we have presented. Refine them, add things, take things away. Notice what shifts for you and find out what works best for you.

Actions I have taken in Part I	✔
Really noticed how I am each day	
Tamed at least one Gremlin	
Worked out my core values	
Taken steps to honour my values more	
Clarified my bigger picture	
Chosen how I want to be with each day – created my saying 'yes' PhD Satnav	
Given myself a celebratory reward for doing everything on this checklist	

Part II

Core themes in the PhD experience

6

Out of control?
In pursuit of better balance

> Guilt is also a way for us to express to others that we are a person of
> good conscience. 'I feel really guilty about getting drunk last night,'
> we say, when in actual fact we feel no guilt whatsoever or, at least, we
> could choose to feel no guilt. When people say to me, 'I drank too
> much last night,' I always reply, 'I drank exactly the right amount.'
> (Tom Hodgkinson, *The Freedom Manifesto*. London:
> Penguin, 2007: 157)

Oh, the burden of doing a PhD! People just don't understand how hard
the responsibility is, especially having to manage your own time: to
have to make decisions about what to focus on, where to work, whether
to take a break or not, when to leave work, whether to say 'yes' to helping
out some students in the lab, some friends on fieldwork, to attend this
training or that. The list of daily dilemmas goes on. Indeed, there is so
much more to doing a PhD than the PhD itself. And there is the rest of
life to fit in as well!

For those who haven't had the privilege of doing a PhD, the burden
might sound like quite an indulgence. For those experiencing the doing
of it, it is so often a real challenge. That challenge comes in different
shapes and forms. Sometimes it appears like a project management
problem: how to coordinate all the things that need to be done (be it for
fieldwork, for literature reviews, for understanding the theory). Other
times it comes in the form of fear: the risk that, if you stop thinking
about it or doing it, you might forget something important (perhaps a

set of ideas, an argument, a flow of thought, or all the things that need to be organized). There are also those moments where it appears as a problem of 'work–life balance': what about the rest of my life, how can I get some of it back? And there are stretches when tensions arise between what needs doing now to get the job done and what needs doing for the future. The list goes on: between finding your voice and writing what you think you should say; doing what you value and doing what you think your supervisor wants you to do; doing that extra bit of work or going for a run . . . time, people, priorities, work and life. In all these situations perhaps what is most alarming is how few role models there are of academics who seem to have got the balance right! How often do you hear someone say 'I did all the preparation I needed to for that presentation', or 'I've read enough on that, don't need to learn more'.

One answer to all this is simple, if hard to accept: 'it's just the nature of the PhD'. Many go with that answer and carry on with their PhD in that way: 'That is how it is.' And perhaps for some people that is just the right thing to do. Our experience suggests otherwise, however, as we pointed out in the Introduction to the book. While we agree there are some peculiarities to doing a PhD, we think – indeed we know – there are some other options here. One choice is to accept it as how the PhD experience is. Another choice – our invitation to you – is to explore alternatives, to see where they might take you, and then choose what works for you. It is an invitation to find the right balance for you. Actually, yes, it *is* hard; for many people, getting a PhD is hard. But that doesn't mean there are no choices in terms of creating a balance.

What are you avoiding taking control of in your life?

What will it mean to you to gain a better balance?

What do you want your balance to say about what you value?

In this chapter we will explore:

- what balance means for you, and what is in and out of balance;
- committing to take small steps towards the balance you want in life and work;

- taking responsibility for your balance over time;
- building up your PhD team: it isn't all down to you.

How are you balanced?

Like it or not, this moment is all we really have to work with.
(Jon Kabat-Zinn, *Wherever You Go, There You Are.*
London: Piatkus 2004: 1)

To think about balance we need to take a snapshot – a snapshot of how satisfied you are, right now, with the balance in your life and in your PhD. So here goes . . .

Challenge: How balanced is your life?

The best way to start is to gain more awareness of what the balance is like for you now. This will help you see some of what is going well rather than just all the doom and gloom. And it will give you a basis for comparison over time.

First, here is a 'balance wheel' for nine different areas of your life. Each could be divided further (e.g. money might be split to cash flow and savings). In each area, ask, 'how satisfied am I?' *at this moment in time.* Give a score between 1 and 10 to reflect your level of satisfaction. 1 is low, 10 is high. With 0 in the centre of the circle, and 10 at the outer edge, draw a line across each segment to reflect your score. Go with your hunch – there is no right answer. It is about how you feel right now, a snapshot (you may feel differently tomorrow or next week). It is not about what others think (friends, family, or colleagues).

Now, look at the wheel, as a whole. What strikes you? If you were riding a bicycle and this was one of your wheels, how would it feel? Would it be smooth? Bumpy? Hard to pedal? Note which areas stand out as needing more attention for you to feel more satisfied, to enjoy the ride!

How does your balance connect with your values? What's at stake here? What really matters?

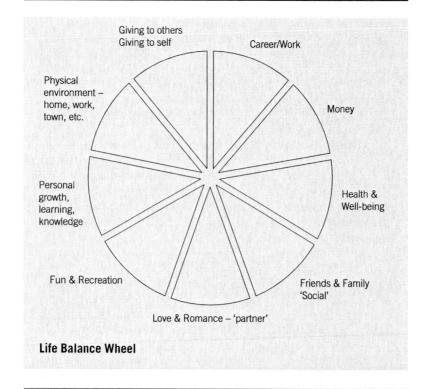

Life Balance Wheel

Brilliant . . . but miserable!

Sheila was a brilliant student. She strove to be the best. Partly she was driven by a fear of failure, and partly she was highly competitive. She was also a perfectionist – which meant that however good she got, and however good the feedback from her supervisor was, she wanted to push herself that bit further. In fact, she came to coaching initially to improve her performance even more, to push herself that much further. Until she stood back for a moment and weighed up her life. Sheila filled in a life balance wheel. Needless to say she was determined to fill it in right, to get the exact right scores! As she started to fill in the different segments with gusto, and with high scores, Sheila suddenly stopped when she got to 'Fun'. Prompted by the coach she said, 'I can't give it a score. Fun has gone out of the window.' Sheila then talked about the other areas. What emerged was that while she'd initially given 'Friends and family' a high score, this was because she felt satisfied because her focus was the PhD. Having reflected on the low score for 'Fun', however, she realized this wasn't the whole truth. What emerged was how miserable she had been feeling, how she spent all her spare time either working on the PhD or swimming to keep fit (needless to say, it was competitive swimming; she had targets!). What emerged for Sheila was that her absolute determination, her competitive streak and perfectionism had made her blank out a part of her life that was really important and that she really valued. That day, Sheila committed to phoning a friend with whom she had lost touch. Over the course of several coaching sessions Sheila managed to find a better balance for herself. She saw more of her friends and family. And she had more fun! Not surprisingly, her work life changed as well. She learnt to stand back from work, to relax more and enjoy a wider life. Sheila found her relationship to the PhD had shifted. While she continued to be driven, and was still competitive and a perfectionist, standing back had enabled her to see a bigger picture of the PhD than before. She actually found herself far more productive and efficient when she was working. She was still a brilliant student, but now a much happier one as well.

Challenge: How balanced is your PhD experience?

So what about your PhD? It may be that the experience of doing it brings a high level of satisfaction in the context of the rest of your life. Even so, when you look at this experience, how balanced is it within that wider context? Here the challenge is to repeat the same process as with the life balance wheel, only this time we focus on the PhD balance wheel.

First, again, give each segment a score of 1 to 10 in terms of your satisfaction. 1 is a low score, 10 is a high score. The segments we have suggested are open for your interpretation. And again this is about how satisfied you feel, not what your supervisor, or peers or anyone else thinks.

Then, look across the wheel as a whole. What stands out? How would the ride feel? Note which areas need more attention for you to feel more satisfied, to enjoy the ride!

Again make connections with your values. What's really important to you about writing, for example, or what matters to you about contributing? Are you aware of any new values as a result of exploring this?

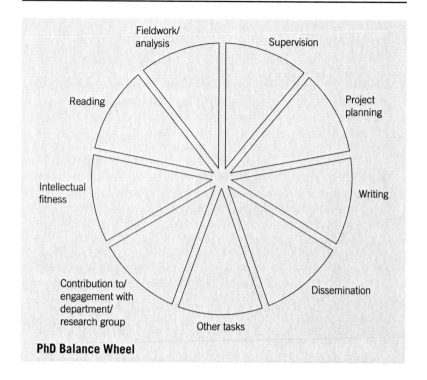

PhD Balance Wheel

Focused, but lacking intellectual fitness

James was an engineer and found, to his surprise, that his life balance wheel was in pretty good shape. Most areas of his life he was reasonably satisfied with, scoring around 8 or 9. The only exception was 'health' where he scored a 6. He said while physically he was very healthy (he played a lot of sport), he often felt an underlying anxiety that he couldn't pin down. He then did the PhD balance wheel and found, again, that most areas were pretty good, scoring between 7 and 9. Two jumped out, though, which scored particularly low: intellectual fitness (3) and engagement with the department (4). James talked about how, while he was satisfied with his reading for his PhD topic, he felt detached from wider debates in his field. When there were seminars, for example, he didn't know what to contribute and couldn't see the relevance. Eventually he'd stopped engaging in departmental seminars and had focused his time and efforts on his PhD. The trouble was, he was struggling to make connections between different parts of his PhD. Having reflected on the wheel, James realized that he needed to look more at his intellectual fitness. Instead of seeing wider activities as a waste of time or irrelevant, he started looking at ways he could keep himself intellectually fit. James decided that he wasn't reading and engaging with wider debates in his discipline, and nor was he exploring different ways of approaching topics. James set up a reading group with the theme 'New directions in engineering' and joined an existing writing group. As well as learning from other people's writing, the reading group also helped set his PhD within the context of wider debates in the discipline. James not only found this inspiring – realizing how his work fits within such debates – he also found himself making connections that he hadn't seen before within his PhD. And, unsurprisingly, he also found himself becoming more actively engaged in the department.

Small steps towards a better balance

Even the journey of a thousand miles began with a single step.
(Chinese proverb, adapted from Lao Tzu,
Tao Te Ching. London: Penguin, 1963[1])

Getting the best balance for you may not be as far away as it seems. Sometimes it may only take a few small steps for you to feel quite different in terms of your level of satisfaction. Indeed, a few small steps, repeated over a period of time, may lead to a significantly different pattern.

Before the next challenge, however, stop to check if there are any Gremlins in the way. They may be pretty obvious ('but it's impossible, I've no time') or disguised as rational planners ('OK, I'll sort this out once I've finished my analysis . . .'). Either way, ditch them (unless you want them to have the last word in your life!). Go back to Chapter 2, if you need to refresh some of your Gremlin-busting skills!

Challenge: Take a step towards a better balance

Getting a better balance is about getting closer to what you value (see Chapter 3).

First, from your life balance wheel, identify one of the areas where you want to improve your satisfaction score. Spend a moment identifying what it is that is missing, and what it is that would make the difference. Now identify a small step that you could take today that would make a difference. That small step could take many different forms, and it may be hard or it may be easy. The key thing is that it is a step towards finding the best balance for you.

For the next week, do something each day towards a better balance.

A small step is all that is required at this moment in time . . . and before you know it . . .

To see the sea . . .

Tony loved the sea. He also loved his PhD. The problem was that the best place for doing his PhD was Birmingham. He couldn't be further from the sort of physical environment that he enjoyed, from places that really inspired him. Over time, his PhD was becoming a burden. He resented the fact that he couldn't live by the sea, take walks on the beach, smell the seaweed, feel the cool breeze. He felt quite trapped. Although at times he felt like giving up the PhD, he also knew it was something he valued. He did want the PhD. What felt like an impossible challenge was shifted when the coach asked, 'How much sea would make you satisfied?' Tony was taken aback. His habit had become to constantly complain, saying that to be happy he needed to live by the sea, to feel and smell it every day. This question suggested something different, that there might be an alternative. The coach pushed a little further: 'At the moment, if you could be by the sea every weekend, would that do it?' After some reflection, a fair amount of Gremlin busting (the Gremlins wanted to stick with 'it's impossible to solve'), and some challenges by numbers (every weekend, once a month, etc.), Tony realized that, actually, what was really important was knowing that he would be with the sea soon, knowing that he had a plan to be by the sea. The outcome of that coaching session was that Tony would, that very day, identify when his next trip to the sea would be and that he would contact a friend to invite them along. Over time, Tony found that a couple of invigorating week-long sea trips each year were enough to give him the 'fix' he needed (coupled with the pictures on his desktop to remind him it wasn't so far away!).

Balance over time

> Life is like riding a bicycle. To keep your balance you must keep moving.
>
> (Albert Einstein, letter to his son Eduard, 5 February 1930,
> quoted by Walter Isaacson, *Einstein: His Life and Universe*.
> New York: Simon & Schuster, 2007: 367)

When you think of balance what does it conjure up? Perhaps you start with a set of traditional weighing scales, in which a weight is used to balance against the ingredients you are measuring. Perhaps you think of an object, finely balanced, perhaps a rock on the edge of a precipice? These may feel rather static and also rather lifeless.

By contrast, picture a bird balancing on the branches of a high tree, a gymnast balancing on a high beam, or a tightrope artist. The balance shifts to something that involves – indeed requires – movement, however tiny that need be. Anyone who has learnt to ride a bike knows how much easier it is to balance on a bicycle when it's moving than when it is standing still. Notice also that balance, like movement, is something that we learn. As babies we don't know how to stand or walk. We have to learn through trial and error. We have to take the bumps, yet we get there in the end.

Gaining control of your PhD and the rest of your life – getting the right balance for you – is not going to be a one-off event. Balance in your PhD experience will involve movement, it will require some learning and some testing of the waters. Whether it is about balancing particular areas of your PhD or particular areas of your life as a whole, how far you want to stretch yourself (and in what areas), is something to explore.

Challenge: Balance over time

The balance wheels are a snapshot offering you a subjective measure as a guide to how you are feeling in the here and now. The next challenge is to do this over time:

- First, choose a date in your diary four weeks ahead.
- Then, on that date, redo your balance wheel scores.
- Next, review your wheels: how do they look compared with the ones you did a month earlier? Is there a pattern? Has something shifted? Is there something new that needs attention?

- Finally, identify some further small steps.

As you review your balance over time, notice how this links with your values. How true do you stay to your values in how you live your life?

Learning to say no . . . and yes!

Feng was a highly talented PhD student in computer science. As well as researching new programming techniques, Feng knew computers and computer systems inside out. He could see the weakness in a system and he couldn't resist offering to find a fix for them. If anyone had a problem, they knew who to ask for help. Over time Feng became indispensable to his colleagues and friends. And over time, well, Feng had very little time. His research began to take a back seat. In his head this wasn't a problem – being indispensable would surely mean, when he finished his PhD, there would be a job for him. After all, they couldn't do without him! An initial coaching session and a look at the balance wheels had revealed that time for relaxing and time for his research were low scorers. However, after several weeks of coaching and having set various 'small steps' to get a better balance, it was clear little had changed. The problem wasn't setting the goals; they were still valid and important. The problem was that all the other demands made of Feng meant he was working all hours and ending up exhausted. With this pattern recurring over a period of weeks, he was eventually able to wake up to the reality of needing to get balance in his life. Feng came up with strategies for saying 'no' to people, including identifying just what it was he was saying 'yes' to when he said 'no'. Saying 'no' to helping a student, re-writing some software or fixing a security threat meant saying 'yes' to his research and his health. In time, it also enabled a new skill to emerge, that is, saying yes to learning to feel comfortable about delegating.

Getting the balance in your perfect PhD team

People come, people go – they'll drift in and out of your life, almost like characters in a favourite book. When you finally close the cover, the characters have told their story and you start up again with another book, complete with new characters and adventures. Then you find yourself focusing on the new ones, not the ones from the past.

(Nicholas Sparks, *The Rescue*. London: Sphere, 2008: 110)

Perhaps it sounds nonsensical to be inviting you to think about balance in your PhD team. Where management gurus might tell you 'there is no "I" in the word team', you might respond, 'but there is an "I" in Doctor of Philosophy'. The PhD is yours, right? After all, ultimately it is down to you to defend your thesis. Once you enter the viva, you are on your own. There are no options to take a chance or phone a friend! That's one perspective. You can choose to stick with this perspective if you think it's helpful. Indeed, for some, the PhD is absolutely about a solo intellectual project that involves very little interaction with, or support from, other people other than their supervisors.

There are alternatives, however. Building the right kind of interactions, support, engagement, and collaboration, including with supervisors, peers, friends, etc., can be just the thing to really get more from the PhD experience. The issue here is partly about nurturing and developing those relationships that enable you to make the contribution you want to make, during the PhD experience. Partly it might also be about starting new relationships where you feel they are currently lacking. There is also a flip side to this, which is letting go or changing those relationships which hinder or drain you. That can be hard. What the author Julia Cameron in *The Artist's Way* (1992) calls 'poisonous playmates', or Marsha Petrie Sue (2007) calls 'Toxic people', or some describe as 'frenemies', are often disguised. The bottom line is they drag us down, stop us feeling good about ourselves, perhaps undermine our sense of confidence.

Whether you want to build up your PhD team, or indeed find yourself needing to downsize, the tricky bit is working out what's possible, and what would be really helpful. Rather like a good spring clean, what would happen if you did a review of your PhD team, i.e. of all the people who are a part of your PhD experience? What if you explored which relationships need starting, developing, changing or even letting go?

Challenge: Your PhD team stocktake

This challenge requires honesty and also recognition that this is a way into thinking about the energy you put into your relationships.

You need Post-it notes and a big piece of paper for this.

First, make a list of all the people who are important to you in your PhD experience. Start with the obvious, such as your supervisors, and include all the people around you who make your life what it is right now (friends, housemates, neighbours, etc.). Write the initials of each person down on a separate Post-it note.

Then draw a graph, i.e. a line across the bottom of the page and a line from the left-hand side of that up towards the top. Put score marks from 1 to 10 along each line. On the vertical axis write 'nurtures'. On the horizontal axis write 'hinders'.

Taking each Post-it note in turn, ask, out of a score of 10 does this person nurture?; and out of 10, does this person hinder? By nurturing we mean people who make you feel good about yourself, energize you, bring out the best in you, feed your spirit. Ask yourself: Would I share my deepest hopes, dreams and fears with this person? Do I trust them with my emotions? By hindering we mean 'grinds me down', i.e. makes you feel bad about yourself, brings out the worst in you, drains you, starves your spirit.

Go with your hunch here. This is not a character evaluation of that person, it is about whether right now you find these people a help or a hindrance.

Place the person on the graph. If they score 10 nurturing and do not hinder at all, place them at the top left-hand side (so a score of 10 and 0). If they are a little nurturing and not at all hindering, place them on the far left, but lower down the nurturing scale, perhaps 2 or 3). If they are nurturing (e.g. score of 7), yet also sometimes hinder (score of 3), place them as appropriate on the graph.

Looking at your graph choose a 'nurturing' relationship which you would like to build on, to make even better. For this relationship ask: How can I spend more quality time with this person? How can I invest more of myself in this relationship? Commit to an action.

Looking at those relationships that are in the 'grinds me down' area of the graph, ask the following:

- What do I lose by keeping this person in my life?
- What is it costing me to be in this relationship?
- What would happen if I stopped seeing this person?
- How would I feel if this person was out of my life for good?
- What am I gaining from this relationship?
- What does being with this person bring out in me?
- How is this person bringing out the best in me?

- How much of myself do I want to invest in this relationship from now on?

Then, consider your answers and choose a 'grinds me down' relationship which if you could improve would significantly benefit you. Ask the following:

- How would improving this relationship help me?
- What do I need to do to shift things (and this may require exploration of further challenges in this chapter)?

A final question to ask of this group is, 'Are there any relationships I need to "drop" altogether?'

Demanding personal relationships

Joe's long-term relationship with his girlfriend had recently broken up and he was finding it difficult to come to terms with this while at the same time struggling to complete the final stages of his PhD. His self-esteem had taken a knock and he was doing less and less productive work. Instead of applying his considerable talents to completing his PhD, he was spending more and more time socializing, including enjoying several quick flings with women he'd met around campus. In particular he spent most time with someone who constantly pressurized him to 'have a good time'. Joe wanted to keep her happy and consequently spent an increasing amount of his time and energy partying and drinking. Hardly surprising then that he was worried about his work. Inspired by a coaching workshop Joe decided to take a long hard look at his network and paid particular attention to the idea of poisonous playmates. He soon realized that while this new girlfriend was filling an empty space in his life, she was doing so in way that didn't fit with his values and didn't nurture his sense of true fulfilment. What he also realized was that while focusing his attention on this person and being in party mode, he had been ignoring other people in his network who were far more supportive of his deeper goals and ambitions. Joe committed to take action and quickly parted company from his new girlfriend. He also phoned two good friends from his undergraduate days that he had lost contact with and arranged to meet them the following weekend.

Note: when thinking about your relationships with your team members, be wary of confusing being challenging with being supportive, don't be fooled. Some people tell you what you want to hear and may make you feel good on the surface but not necessarily good deep down in your 'essence' or 'spirit'. You may even question their true motives in doing this. In many cases your true 'friends' are those who, with sound intentions, will ask you that difficult question or confront you with a hard home truth. You may not feel good at the time, but in the long run the challenge they pose for you is nurturing.

Note also, we don't often think in these ways about relationships and this may raise some tricky or uncomfortable issues. For example it's not unusual to find poisonous playmates among our close or extended family – we can choose our friends but can't choose our relatives! Sometimes a complete break from someone is the best way forwards and at other times we may feel this isn't appropriate or even possible. If that's the case, then look to see what can be achieved in other ways. Perhaps by spending less time with someone, committing less energy to the relationship or setting ground rules for how they behave towards us. These can mean an awkward conversation and as a consequence we may go through life avoiding it. However, the need for these important conversations doesn't go away by ignoring them. Chapter 11 offers some tools for help in this direction.

You may at this point also need to check what new relationships you might want to start up. Sometimes we put a lot of pressure on a particular relationship when there may be options to engage with other people. Perhaps your partner doesn't have to be your PhD moaning board? Could it be that your supervisor isn't the only person who can give you the constructive feedback you need? Are there networks of researchers beyond your department that can engage in your work? Is it possible you need to meet up with new people to have fun and stimulation beyond university life?

Supervisory overload

Probably many jokes could be made about how many supervisors it takes to change a light bulb! For Katie, the problem of having four supervisors was no laughing matter. Her supervisors were not used to working together, her PhD was the first time they had tried to collaborate. They were all strong-minded. They all had opinions about what Katie should be prioritizing, even when her focus was outside of their specialty. Not only did Katie find she had few supervisory meetings, when she met with all of them, it was overwhelming and intimidating as they all seemed to compete with each other to get their points across (as well as apparently score points!). She tried meeting each individually, only then she found herself pulled in very different directions. Katie thought about her PhD team. As a cycling fan, she imagined herself as the lead rider of a cycling team in the Tour de France and thought about what she needed to win the yellow jersey. Using that analogy, Katie identified what input and support she felt she needed to keep on top of her PhD. She mapped out the work involved and started to match people to the jobs that she'd identified. Katie decided that there was one supervisor whom she felt could play a really good central role, someone she could see regularly and who could understand the bigger picture of the PhD. She then mapped the other supervisors to particular parts of the PhD that reflected their expertise. Turning her work into a PhD project plan, Katie realized that some of the supervisors would be needed at different times for specific input. She also realized there were gaps where she could draw on other people. Katie built up some confidence and decided to approach her favoured 'lead' supervisor. Together they agreed to present the plan to the others. Despite Katie's Gremlin voice that told her she'd be upsetting people and they would dismiss her, they were all delighted! They said this meant they could use their time to help her much more effectively and that they would get more out of it.

Challenge: Building up your PhD team

Although some people are quite tricky, the vast majority of people love to cooperate. People like to make a contribution. In this challenge we want you to review your PhD team specifically in relation to supervision.

First of all, take someone you sometimes find helpful and also at other times find a hindrance. Ask yourself: what am I expecting this person to contribute to the team? Write down your list of expectations. Second, ask yourself, who else might be able to make that contribution? Look at other 'team' members and see if you might be able to draw on them (or enable them to make more of a contribution).

Then, think about all the things involved in your PhD experience. This means both looking at the detail of the PhD itself and also the wider network of activities that enable you to have the experience you want. Are there gaps where you feel you need more support?

Who might fill those gaps? This might be about existing people in your PhD team, however, it might also involve bringing in more team players.

Identify what actions you need to take to build up your team. This may involve some tricky conversations with your supervisors, a basis for which you'll find in Chapter 11.

Note: it's a common PhD condition to feel let down by your supervisor. It may well be the case that some difficult conversations need to be had with your supervisor, and Chapter 11 will help with that. However, it's also possible that you could take some responsibility for your expectations. In looking at building up your PhD team it may be that you need to take a closer look at the role of supervision. What role are you expecting your supervisor to play: line manager, sounding board, mentor, advisor, expert, coach, boss, director, friend, colleague, counsellor, director, practitioner, career advisor? Who else could fulfil some of those roles? Be creative here and look within your department, your peers, the university, the wider research community, people beyond academia, etc. With the internet your PhD team could span the globe.

The research community

Martina wanted to undertake a complex study design that involved drawing on some very different types of knowledge as well as types of lab experiments. Despite long conversations with her supervisor and other people in a similar area of work at the university, she wasn't getting very far. It was a frustrating experience. After some months of getting nowhere Martina decided that perhaps she would have to think about a wider PhD team. She knew there was a community of researchers across other universities who were interested in the ideas she was working on, though they were applying them in a different context to her. Plucking up her courage, Martina decided to send an email to the network explaining what she wanted to do and the difficulties she was having. To her surprise, two people responded that afternoon! One explained how there was some lab equipment that could go some way to helping her get over some of the obstacles. The other said that this was really exciting work and invited her to present at a workshop they were organizing where she could meet up with various people working in this area. She did so and to her and her supervisor's excitement, they took the research even further than they expected and had an article accepted in a prestigious journal.

Next steps to a better balance

Achieving balance is a process; being in balance itself is a process. It is a process through which what we do aligns with what we value, with what matters to us. In that sense, balance is about satisfaction.

The challenges we have set out in this chapter have been ones that try to capture your sense of satisfaction now, in this moment, and which invite you, challenge you, to make some small steps toward increasing your satisfaction. We've also invited you to explore that over time. This has been a small step. There may be more small steps to take, or some larger ones.

There are some other chapters in the book that can help with this:

- It may be that you lack confidence to take the steps you want to take towards a better balance (see Chapter 7).
- Perhaps you are struggling to find creative ideas for the steps you want to take (see Chapter 9).
- You may be having trouble setting goals, big and small, that keep you motivated and on the right path (see Chapter 8).
- Sometimes, if things have been out of balance for a long time, there is a need to build up some resilience (see Chapter 12).
- The balance may require a conversation with someone else (see Chapter 11).
- Better balance might be about looking beyond your PhD, towards your authenticity (see Chapter 13).
- Finally, it may be you need to look back to Part I and review your Gremlins, your values, your bigger picture and a routine to saying 'yes' to the perfect PhD day . . .

Note

1   The direct quotation is 'A journey of a thousand miles starts from beneath one's feet', however, this adaptation is commonly used (Lao Tzu 1963: Book 2, Chapter 64, p. 71, line 157).

Actions I have taken in this chapter	✔
Taken a snapshot and reviewed balance in my life	
Taken a snapshot and reviewed balance in my PhD	
Taken a small step towards a better balance in my life	
Taken a small step towards a better balance in my PhD	
Set a future date in my diary to review my balance again	
Reviewed my PhD team and taken actions to develop it	
Identified which chapters of the book might be the most helpful	
Given myself a balanced reward for doing everything on this checklist	

7

When self-doubt creeps in . . . how to find the superhero within

It's true most superheroes have funny names. But they have to come up with these names by themselves. Think about how hard it is. Try it, right now; boil down your personality and abilities to a single phrase or image. If you can do that, you're probably a superhero already.

(Andrew Kaufman, *All My Friends Are Superheroes*. London: Telegram Books, 2006: 73)

There is a certain irony within the academic world that can perhaps be summed up by the phrase 'feeling like a fraud'. The irony is that other people often expect those doing PhDs to feel at the top of their game. After all, if you are doing a PhD you must surely be a pioneer, in command of your field and pushing at the frontiers of knowledge! So why do PhD students – many academics, actually – often feel like a fraud, feel as if one day they might just be 'found out', worried that some day their peers and colleagues, as well as the world 'out there', will find out that it has all been a big misunderstanding, that the qualifications you achieved through your schooling and education were all just a fluke and that, in fact, everyone should just realize you're really not up to this PhD business?

Oh, how the evidence floods in when you are in that mood! It comes in all sorts of shapes and forms. At its worst, a spiral of paranoia envelopes your view of the world, while at other times the self-doubt can just be a tingling that nonetheless holds us back from enjoying the ride and pushing that bit further. Let's be honest here. There is always plenty of evidence in universities to demonstrate you are not good enough. There are always people much better at thinking, writing, arguing, presenting, calculating, theorizing, doing fieldwork, being organized, managing emails, asking questions and even having fun! To really rub it in, the institution is built up around creating situations where we can be absolutely sure of that. We give presentations in which colleagues quiz us about why we did what we did, write papers for supervisors or peer reviewers to knock down, and have to defend – defend! – our work in a viva. So there is some truth in the notion that the work you are producing could always have been better, pushed a little further, may prove to be wrong, and it may turn out you took a wrong turning.

So can we find an alternative route, a route that builds our self-confidence? Let's start off with a different version to the account above. Let's shift from the glass half-empty to a glass half-full, filling up and effervescent! A view in which, of course, we cannot know everything, we could have done more, there were other ways to do it and, of course, we may have made mistakes. A view in which we want to put it all out there in presentations, in writing, supervision and in a viva because, of course, we want to share what we have learnt and we know it's the best we could make it within the boundaries we have defined. And of course there is always someone else who might have done it better, differently, more successfully. And, yes, that is the very reason some people find it so exciting. You needn't share this view. You can create your own. Our invitation is to create a view that helps you see and explore the contribution you are making and to find your superhero within!

In this chapter we offer ways for:

- tapping into your 'super hero' and feeling confident;
- acknowledging and doing what buoys you up and stop doing what brings you down;
- unlocking the rebel within by challenging some rules;
- putting 'you' first.

What will you gain as your confidence grows?

What do you do that undermines your own confidence?

What will being more confident say about you as a person?

Being your confident superhero, despite and with everything else!

> No one can make you feel inferior without your permission.
> (Attributed to Eleanor Roosevelt, source unknown)

The idea of building your own sense of self-confidence may seem a little arrogant. Shouldn't our confidence come from getting good feedback from our supervisors on what we are doing, or perhaps when we see our first words in print, or people say they enjoyed our presentation? That is when we should feel confident. Of course, all of that is great and such moments are good to celebrate. However, it's a fine line to tread, since it follows that when we don't get such good feedback, our confidence may start to ebb. Following this logic, our confidence is out of our own hands. A risky business in an academic world set up to critique whatever is said or written!

Let's try a different take on confidence, one that starts with a sense of self-assurance and goes something like: whatever happens, I'll be OK. Whatever happens, I can handle it. Whatever happens, I've stuck to what matters to me and done the best I felt able to do in the time I had. Whatever I hear back about this piece of work, I've been true to myself. It's a switch to finding a place of confidence within yourself, an inner belief in your abilities, a confidence based on self-belief, a confidence to be able to handle whatever comes your way. It's a confidence that you can do it, and that even if you don't, you'll learn something important along the way. That's the challenge here: how to feel confident, despite and with everything around!

Challenge: Create a feeling of confidence

This is an exercise to help you tap into that feeling of being confident and involves remembering a peak experience.

Before you start, choose a simple gesture that you can use to connect with being confident. This is sometimes called a trigger or anchor. For some, it's holding their hands together in a particular way, for others clenching their fist, for others squeezing their thumb and middle finger. You choose.

1 Think back to a time when you felt really confident. Perhaps a time during your PhD, or your degree, or when you were doing something completely different. What's important is not what happened before, or after, rather the very moment when you felt most confident.
2 Remember that moment vividly. Bring it alive. What were you doing? Who was around you? What were you wearing? What could you see? What could you hear? How did you feel? What sensations were you feeling in your body?
3 Stay in the moment and allow your sense of confidence to intensify. Try making the images brighter and more colourful. Make the sounds louder and crisper. See what works for you. Notice your physiology associated with being confident, how are you standing, what position your head is in, your shoulders, back, etc.
4 Now, keeping that sense of confidence and holding your physiology of confidence, notice the image that comes to mind that really connects you to that sense of confidence?
5 Keeping the feeling of confidence strong and the image in your mind's eye, make and hold the gesture you chose at the beginning. If you need to, repeat any of the steps above.

To access your state of being confident, you now have two triggers: an image and a physical gesture. Like any new skill, this may take practice and you might want to set a goal of practising this every day for two weeks.

The power of acting 'as if'

Caleb was really nervous about a presentation he had to do at a conference. His anxiety had to do with feeling a little unsure about some of his analysis. He felt a fraud, that he was going to be 'found out' and that he would mess up the presentation – a sort of stage fright. Know that feeling? There was no time before the presentation to do more analysis. Pulling out would be one option, and yet he really wanted the feedback and debate about the ideas. It was a Catch-22 situation. Caleb's solution was simple: it was to act *as if* he was confident. Caleb had a routine he'd developed to tap back into his confidence zone: it was linked to playing music when he felt really in the flow. His trick was to imagine he was holding the pick to his guitar. He brought this sense of confidence to approach the presentation. He had done presentations well in the past, so he knew how it feels to present with confidence. He was also inspired by presenters like the late Steve Jobs, the founder of Apple Computers, so he knew what an interesting presentation could look like. He spent some moments reminding himself what it *felt like* to do a good presentation with confidence and how he wanted the presentation to be. Caleb went on to do a fantastic presentation *as if* he felt confident about his work: he engaged the audience and people thanked him for it. He also got some fantastic feedback about his analysis and how to improve it. Just what he wanted!

Generating the habits of your inner superhero

We are what we repeatedly do.
Excellence, then, is not an act, but a habit.
(Aristotle, cited by Stephen Covey, *The 7 Habits of Highly Effective People: Powerful Lessons in Personal Change*, 2nd edn. New York: Simon & Schuster 2004: 47)

When we speak of habits, we tend to think of all the negative connotations they bring up: bad habits. Habits are something to be stopped. Think of children biting their fingernails or sucking their thumb, or adults who go straight for the coffee to wake up. Habits, though, are also what get us through life – and through our PhDs! If we had to think consciously of everything we did each day, that would be quite a chore, or indeed impossible. So surely all habits can't be bad? It follows that we need to take this a little further.

Are there habits that do more than just get us through? Are there habits that can help to build our sense of confidence? Are there habits that could bring us confidence in our writing, our reading, in our conversations with peers, in negotiations with supervisors, in preparing for our viva, in thinking about the future? Following Aristotle's suggestion, can we start to find habits, things we do repeatedly, that can build our sense of being confident?

Challenge: Identify your uppers and downers

Just to be clear: we're not talking controlled substances here! Over a period of three days note which of your habits are uppers (boost confidence) and which habits are downers (drain confidence). You might want to do this as a table with habits in one column, and the impact on your mood in the other. Or you might want to keep a diary or create a mind-map. You can be creative about that. The key thing is to create a log of the habits that make you feel confident and good about yourself, and those that don't.

Some tips on this: habits are things that we repeat, well, 'habitually', and so often go unnoticed. Spotting them may require a bit more reflection than normal. Habits come in all sorts of shapes and forms so here are some tips for things you might want to look at:

- habits of thoughts or day dreams;
- habits of debriefing after meetings or at the end of the day;
- habits of eating and drinking;
- habits of conversation;
- habits of what we prioritize;
- habits of how we start our day;
- habits of who we spend time with;
- habits of when we take breaks and what we do with them;
- habits of planning the day and setting goals;
- habits of what we do, and what we put off;
- habits of what we wear;
- habits around personal care;
- habits of how we relax;
- habits of what we say to ourselves.

That's a lot of habits and it's down to you to work out which boost your confidence and which don't. We want to open up the possibility that you could make changes.

Now, looking at your list of uppers and downers, your 'habit-confidence map', the question is what to do with it.

Challenge: Do more of your uppers and less of your downers!

This might seem obvious but making it happen is perhaps another thing! There are two steps to this challenge:

- First, set a clear goal for yourself. We'd suggest you start by identifying one particular noisy 'downer' that you are going to stop, and one particularly quiet 'upper' that you'd like to make louder. Changing your habit is about to become a 'goal', something you want to achieve with an end in sight, to be more confident. You might want to reflect on Chapter 8 on goal setting to think more about how to set that goal.
- Then, create a structure to stop the old and bring in the new. Habits are often so structured into our daily routines, shifting a habit can mean changing those structures. Those structures might come in the form of where you do things, who you do things with, when you do things and for how long, about the things you have around you when you are doing, or thinking, them. Imagine trying to give up chocolate if you always have chocolate on your desk, hang around with people who always eat lots of chocolate, and don't find something to replace it with (perhaps some nuts!). In other words, why not make it easier for yourself to create these new habits?

Talking habits

Ben started his day feeling really confident. He'd worked out each day what his goals were, he had got pretty good in the mornings at getting himself in the right mood for the work ahead of him, and usually achieved a core goal each morning before 11 a.m. before switching on his email. At that point he'd often also catch up with his office pals over a coffee. That was when his day started to go a little wrong. He realized that those conversations over coffee had become a really negative space, a space in which they would all moan, including Ben, about the problems of supervisors, about how the university doesn't value them, about how disappointing the seminar speaker was, etc. All valid points, all with some truth in them. And all points of conversation that lead Ben to feeling a sense of heaviness, anxiety and 'What's the point?' Worse still, at the end of the day he realized his conversation with his partner tended to relaying all the negativity of the day. Ben's partner got to the point of saying, 'Look, just do something different if it's that bad, get a job or something instead.' That was a shock for Ben because he valued his PhD and didn't want to give it up. And he valued his partner. He realized that, actually, he could stop the negative conversations. He played a little game with himself.

Whenever a negative conversation started up, he'd say, 'Hey, guess what, this morning, I . . .' and then ask the others what they had done. He also made sure, when he came home, that he only spoke about the things he felt good about during the day to his partner. Over time, the positive conversations became a new habit and Ben kept his confidence through the day. Now, of course all the bad stuff had not gone away. What had gone away was just the habit of talking about it. He also found there were times he did want to talk about problems at work, and when he did so he did it with more purpose and in a more constructive way. Interestingly, the PhD group he was a part of starting thinking about what they might do to change some of the issues with supervisors and their own contributions to the university too.

Changing habits can be really hard and can involve all sorts of diversions. Perhaps we all have some sort of 'road block' Gremlin. Stephen Covey writes, 'I have personally found living the 7 habits a constant struggle – primarily because the better you get, the very nature of the challenge changes' (2004: 12). Indeed, how often have you found yourself putting off or avoiding the very thing that you know you want to do, and which might make you feel more confident? How often have you found yourself engaging in self-deflating habits, finding comfort in the familiar and routine, even if you know it's not good for you? If changing a particular habit is a struggle, then it's worth shifting up a level and going back to questions about what it is that really matters here for you. The tools in Chapter 3 will help in this, in particular those that are about really honing in on what you value and bringing that to the centre stage of what you do in you PhD experience.

At this point, then, with practice, you've hopefully found from the first set of challenges in this chapter an ability to tap into your sense of being confident, and from this second set of challenges some new habits, and structures to support them, that help boost your confidence in your PhD. So, now anything is possible . . .

Letting your superhero rebel

How much more there is now to living! Instead of our drab slogging forth and back to the fishing boats, there's a reason to life! We can lift ourselves out of ignorance, we can find ourselves as creatures of excellence and intelligence and skill. We can be free! We can learn to fly!

(Richard Bach, *Jonathan Livingston Seagull*. New York: Macmillan, 1970: 17)

The story of Jonathan Livingston Seagull is about a seagull who wants more from life than his fellow seagulls. To get more from living, to experience fulfilment, he first learns to break the rules, to go beyond the boundaries of what is allowed, to learn to fail and to persevere. To learn to do so despite the pressures from the 'flock' to conform, to do what is expected, to be an average seagull. Jonathan had an inner confidence and inner belief through which he overcame the 'rules' of the flock. The question to which we turn here is: what self-imposed rules are you working to that you need to break out from? Not so much the rules of the flock – we're not suggesting you break any laws here! Rather, those rules that can become straitjackets to your PhD experience. What rules do you impose on yourself that shape your PhD experience?

Some of our self-imposed rules may well seem like habits but they are more intentional and tend to use the language of our oh-so-lovely Gremlin friends. They may be habits that have turned to rules because we feel we 'should', 'must', 'have to', 'ought'. . . . We mustn't break these habits, then, because they are a rule. Rules are habits with attitude! Some of these rules may have been really handy at some point in time. Whether they still are is another question. Perhaps they have passed their sell-by date and need composting!

Challenge: Learning to rebel!

First, what 'self-imposed rules' do you habitually follow? You might want to think in general terms here, as we have done in the list below, or you might want to look at some specific area of your PhD, like writing or reading.

- Checking emails first thing.
- Having coffee before I can start work.
- Needing a shower before I can wake up.
- Can only focus on writing between 5 and 7 p.m.
- Seeking reassurance from others before making a decision.
- Having fish for dinner on Fridays.

- Getting drunk Saturday night.
- Never going to bed before midnight.
- Never making quick decisions.
- Always visiting in-laws at Christmas.
- Cigarette or cup of coffee to think.
- Putting petrol on credit cards.
- Never being the first to speak.
- Never going first.
- Always going along with what others think or want.
- Putting children first.
- Putting partners first.
- Doing the washing-up the next day.
- Hoovering on a Saturday.
- Always writing at my desk.
- Always doing what I'm told.
- Glass of wine to relax.

The question is, do these rules serve you well or not? For sure, they may all have been useful at some point, but which still work well for you now? Which really honour your values? Which ones work well *in relation to your priorities at the moment*? For example, checking email first thing in the morning. If your priority at the moment is coordinating with stakeholders to undertake fieldwork, perhaps it's just the thing you need to do to check the email first thing and regularly through the day. Perhaps, though, checking email first thing, or even having it on all day, has become more than a bit of a habit and is now a rule, something you feel you 'must do', before you give yourself permission to tackle your priorities. So, it's not about rights or wrongs as judged by someone else, it's about you deciding what is working for you in line with your values, bigger picture and priorities.

Pick a rule that is not serving you well, that isn't helping any more and . . . commit to breaking it! How does it feel making this commitment? Does it feel scary? Exciting? Obvious? Liberating? Are you wondering why you have waited so long to give yourself permission to rebel?

Consider the rules that you think still serve you well. Go through the list and try this for size: 'If I were to replace that rule with something else, what might it be?' Try the replacement on, and see what happens. You may learn you have other options, or you may confirm that it is just what you need. Just to give one example: taking a shower to wake up. Perhaps a short walk around the block or in the nearby park could serve just as well? Could the new possibility even open something else up?

Must have a 'to do' list

Miao was a great planner. One of her rules was to make sure everything was on a list and that everything on that list had a time and place to get it done. The planning bit was great, she always felt in control and able to see just what needed doing by when. Doing it was another matter. Ironically, this would create a lot of stress. Why? Because, of course, new jobs and tasks would emerge. Miao got caught in a trap. Learning and exploring – the very essence of doing the PhD for her – meant new things would crop up. These new things might not fit the plan, and yet her hunch would be to follow them. Having got in a muddle and become considerably anxious, a friend said to her, 'Miao, you know this is how it is, so why not try something different?' Something different! At first, she resisted; she needed to write the plans to know what to do. Still in a state and again sharing a drink with this friend (who'd done some coaching training!), the friend said, 'Look, what you've been doing isn't working, is it? So you could stick with that – or not. Perhaps the question is this: how do you want to be with knowing that new things emerge? Perhaps you need to find another way of being with your work?' This made Miao think. She realized she wanted to be excited about new things emerging and to be able to follow hunches. Following that through, she realized that what she needed was a sense of organization and one that was a little more fuzzy, less rigid and more adaptable. The rule of 'write the plan first' was abandoned and replaced with 'get the vision right first', then prioritize the day with the important things first. Over time Miao became more productive, she got her core jobs done while other things came and went, and small jobs got done really efficiently.

So, see what happens to your confidence when you give yourself permission to break some rules or try on some new ones. In what follows we're really going to push that rebel . . .

Being selfish and putting you first!

You yourself, as much as anybody in the entire universe, deserve your love and affection.

(Attributed to Buddha, source unknown)

Part of building confidence during your PhD as well as during life in general can be about making sure your own needs are met. That can be so hard to hear, let alone accept and put into practice. Not least because, for many people, doing a PhD can feel like such a selfish and self-obsessed endeavour. There can be so much resistance to the idea of putting yourself first because it comes so close to being 'selfish'. So you might need your rebel with you here – and, of course, your super-hero!

We are not talking here about being selfish in any conventional sense of the word. After all, wouldn't it be fair to say that, when you are at your best, feeling the most confident, you are probably able to give more to others? After all, what makes you so special that you should not receive the attention you might want to give to others? Indeed, if you don't refuel yourself, how can you expect to be able to offer fuel to others? Might it be the case that it is through confidence in your own independence – a confidence in what you are doing and why you are doing it and that isn't based on seeking reassurance or acceptance from others – that you can forge much more powerful, authentic and sincere relationships and interdependencies? It's always a challenge, for example, to be really honest with ourselves and ask: when we are 'helping' someone else, or putting them first, who are we *really* doing this for?

Let's remember that this book is based on coaching philosophy, and coaching is about trying things out and seeing what works for you. So, rather than dwell on debates around the ethics of putting yourself first, what we suggest is you try some things out and see what you learn about yourself, your priorities in your PhD, and your relationships with others.

Challenge: Who are you doing this for?

This is based on a simple continuum with 'self-fulfilment' at one end and 'approval of others' at the other. Try this by drawing a continuum with a note at one end saying 'Self-fulfilment' and a note at the other saying 'Approval from others'.

Self-fulfilment--Approval from others

Now, if you think about how you are approaching a part of your PhD experience – this may be something specific to the PhD (writing, reading, supervision), or it may be about the PhD in your wider setting (friends, family, etc.) – where would you put yourself on the continuum? Now, keeping the area you have chosen in focus, move your approach more towards the 'approval from others' end of the line. How does that impact on your confidence? And then move towards the doing things for 'self-fulfilment' end of the line. How does that make you feel? What happens to your confidence there? In each case, go all the way to the end, take it to the extreme and test it out.

In relation to how you are approaching this part of your PhD (decisions you are making, etc.), where would you like to be on the line? Where would be the best place for your confidence?

Let's be clear here: we are not saying that all your decisions must be at the self-fulfilment end. For some decisions during your PhD, it's going to be really important to get the approval of others, for example, passing a confirmation panel, or even the viva! They require the approval of others! However, what we are encouraging is for you to check with yourself how far you are compromising yourself in the decisions, habits and rules you are producing during your PhD and so undermining your own confidence. When faced with a decision about what to write, or a request from someone to help with something, it might be useful to ask, who am I doing this for, with what motive, and with what impact on myself (and others)?

No doubt the 'guilt' factor is playing large for some readers, too. It's often said that 'guilt' is a wasted emotion, one that often doesn't lead us anywhere. It's possible that a Gremlin has popped up for you. You 'ought not' . . . in which case, do the tricks that work for you from Chapter 2. Life without 'guilt' can be so enabling!

It may be that you are feeling a conflict, a sense of friction between the idea of putting yourself first rather than putting others first in order to seek their approval. Perhaps pushing towards the 'Self-fulfilment' end feels like there is a conflict with one of your core values? Be careful here about what we mean. Doing something to seek 'approval' from others is quite different from doing something for others. We often talk about finding the 'win–win' situation. In this sense, perhaps you can be moving towards the self-fulfilment end of the line *while at the same time* meeting the needs of others. What that means, though, is not meeting the needs of others because you are seeking their approval (or avoiding their disapproval) but because meeting their needs is something you value in itself.

Bother your supervisor!

Sally was desperate to talk with her supervisor for several weeks about some problems she was having with her data analysis. She really felt she couldn't move forward until she got some help. However, Sally could see her supervisor was really busy and really stressed and so kept putting off approaching him, convincing herself she would work through it. When she got really stuck, a friend confronted her. At first, Sally said she didn't want to bother her supervisor. Her friend pushed a little further and Sally admitted she was worried her supervisor would think she was stupid (avoiding disapproval) for not being able to resolve it. Pushed along by her friend, Sally admitted that, actually, it was really important to her to get this data moving ahead. She also realized that it was her supervisor's job to help, and that he could decide about his priorities and time for himself. Indeed, her friend (being cruel to be kind) said how dare she assume responsibility for her supervisor. In the end, Sally approached the supervisor. He was so relieved. Not only had he been so busy with administrative demands that this was a chance to engage with something he felt mattered; he was also really impressed that Sally had identified a very important issue that could have been easily overlooked.

Next steps to being confident

What we've offered you in this chapter are some core ways of tapping into your confidence right now. Themes in other chapters will also contribute to building your confidence (for example, through getting things done, getting a better balance and building your resilience). Building confidence takes practice, though. You can't become a confident long distance runner immediately, yet you can feel confident of your running abilities right now and build from there. So, being confident is about knowing what you are capable of now and knowing that you can be capable of more in the future. It's about knowing that you do have a superhero within you! Following the exercises in this chapter is just a start, indeed, other chapters will take you further. What you now need is to commit to doing those things that build up your superhero within. What things will you do each day that will build your self-confidence?

In fact, what if you simply reminded yourself each day of all your achievements and successes?

Actions I have taken in this chapter	✓
Tapped into my feeling of being confident using a peak experience	
Taken steps to do more of my confidence uppers and less of my downers	
Created a structure to help me change my habits	
Broken a self-imposed rule that isn't helping me any more	
Replaced an old rule with one that is more useful	
Taken steps to get more of my own needs met	
Identified areas from other chapters that will help boost my confidence	
Given myself a confidence-building reward for doing everything on this checklist	

8

Overwhelmed or underwhelmed?

Finding enjoyment through your goals

> Enjoyment appears at the bou ndary between boredom and anxiety, when the challenges are just balanced with the person's capacity to act.
>
> (Mihaly Csikszentmihalyi, *Flow: The Psychology of Happiness: The Classic Work on How to Achieve Happiness*, new edn, London: Rider, 2002: 52)

We all have goals, even if we don't like the word. Getting a PhD is presumably one of yours if you are reading this book? However, setting goals in a way that keeps you motivated and enables you to find enjoyment is something of an art. The PhD is a difficult beast, and it's made more difficult if we leave it as one big thing that one day will get done. It's also made more difficult if we claim somehow that the creativity of our intellectual work cannot possibly be reduced to something as mundane as strategies for goal setting. Yet we suggest it can. In fact, we suggest you are already doing it. Everyone doing a PhD has a goal at some level. What we do in this chapter is invite you to explore ways of finding the right balance between overwhelm (i.e. this is all too much) and underwhelm (i.e. this is boring).

Overwhelm in the PhD can come in different guises: the thought that your task is to make a contribution to knowledge; awareness of the vast and growing literature already written relevant to your topic; the thought of having to sift through all your data and analysis; 60,000+ words to write over three or more years; not enough time to do all you need to do to get the research done properly; having to speak to world experts in your field when you know so little; being overwhelmed by a sense of perfectionism, by the pressure to perform, by a sense of constant anxiety; worries about how to do those extra bits to get a job afterwards. And so on.

At the same time, the PhD can also be an experience of underwhelm: realizing your findings will not make a huge dent on existing bodies of knowledge and are unlikely to lead to world peace or a Nobel Prize; the boredom of collecting, sorting and analysing data and organizing bibliographies; the monotony of writing up your results for days on end; feeling 'stuck' with a problem for weeks on end; reading endless papers on the same topic for months on end; a lack of stimulating discussion in your department; discovering your supervisors have their failings too; finding it all just a little too easy; discovering that university life is not for you and wondering 'what next?'

> What would it mean to you to be more passionate about what you are doing?
>
> How fulfilled do you feel at the end of each day?
>
> What do your goals say about you?

Somewhere between overwhelm and underwhelm is the place where we keep ourselves motivated, even when doing a PhD. That is the place we invite you to find, and to do so by engaging with some questions about goal setting and turning your goals into actions.

In this chapter we steer you towards the following challenges:

- identifying where you want to set some goals;
- exploring what it is that matters about that goal area, what's the point?
- getting beyond the predictable and asking 'what is possible?'
- getting SMART about your goals;
- working out what is the stretch, what is your limit and what's enough?

Obvious maybe, but where do you want to set some goals?

There seems something so obvious about setting a goal and yet, at the same time, when we ask PhD students in coaching sessions 'what's the goal here?' it's surprising how often it's not clear. To give you some focus to this chapter, you need to spend some time thinking about an area of your PhD experience where it would be useful to set clearer goals.

There may be a particular piece of work that you need to complete – perhaps some writing or fieldwork or data analysis? Perhaps a presentation you have looming over you? If you know what your goal is, that's great, move on to the next section.

You may feel less clear. Perhaps it's all one big mess. If you feel like this, then we suggest you take a look at the balance wheels we introduced in Chapter 6. There we introduced two balance wheels, one for 'life' and one for the PhD. Reflecting on the wheels, pick out an area that would be useful to work on during this chapter. You can work through other areas later, though we suggest you do this one at a time.

It may also be that your 'goal' is not so much about the doing of your PhD and is more about your confidence, creativity, resilience, or about relationships. All of these areas can also benefit from some goal setting, in which case you may want to review those chapters first. At the same time, it might be that setting a specific PhD goal will help in these areas. As you achieve your goals, your self-confidence will grow. Knowing what your goals are – and which goalposts are moveable – could also be important to your resilience when you suffer the inevitable setbacks.

Examples of areas for goal setting

- Complete the thesis as soon as possible.
- Feel more confident with doing presentations.
- Develop a better relationship with my supervisor.
- Become more efficient at getting things done.
- Create more 'down time'.
- Get a better balance between the PhD and the rest of life.

- Feel good about my writing.
- Handle criticism from my supervisors.
- Have more fun.
- Feel more committed to the PhD process.
- Open up some career opportunities.
- Find ways to become more creative
- . . . .

Before you move on, though, make sure you have a goal of some kind . . .

But what's the point?

Do you ever have those moments in your PhD where it's just not happening and you hear yourself say, in a child-like voice, 'What's the point?'. Actually, it might be worth a little Gremlin check moment: are there any lurking here? Any saying, 'What's the point?', or 'Can't see how you can set goals for writing, or reading, or fieldwork', or saying, 'Come on, you haven't got time for this reflection business'? Your goal setting is going to work better without the help of these loyal friends. If they are about, use the tools from Chapter 2 and put them aside for a while.

Before we go any further, you need to make sure that at some level you know why you are reading this chapter! There isn't really an option just to go through the motions here. Well, there is, and you can. However, if you do that, what you'll end up with is a slightly more nuanced, justified, and perhaps more glorified 'to do' list than you have right now. What you will not get without some moments of reflection and engagement are goals that are going to shift your sense of motivation and enjoyment of the PhD experience. The question here is: What's at stake for you in getting the right goal? What is the point?

Challenge: Why? Why? And why?

We need you to turn the child-like 'What's the point?' into a still child-like 'why . . . why . . . why?' And to have the curiosity of an inquisitive, potentially annoying, child that always asks 'why?' to the answer you give to any question.

First, taking whatever goal you have at the moment, ask, 'Why is this important to me?'

Write down your answer.

Now, to whatever answer you gave, ask, 'Why is *this* important to me?' And again, until you've done it at least six times.

And then a final question based on your penultimate answer: 'What will it mean to me when I achieve this?'

Look at the next box. If you have asked why, why and why, and if you have been honest with yourself, you'll now have a sense of how setting the right goal for yourself is important. You will know what the point is!

Why, why, why . . . reading around the subject

Jane was feeling unmotivated because she didn't feel her PhD was important to anyone. Her particular focus seemed irrelevant to everyone else in her department. On reflection, Jane realized that part of the challenge was a need to understand the wider context of her work and how her work fitted into the bigger debates. She did the exercise above as follows:

Question: Why is reading around the subject important to me?
Answer: *Because I need a broader understanding of debates in the subject.*

Question: Why is having a broader understanding important to me?
Answer: *Because it will be easier to see how my PhD might contribute to those debates.*

Question: Why is making a contribution important to me?
Answer: *Because the PhD feels pointless at the moment.*

Question: Why is not feeling pointless important to me?
Answer: *Because I start to get fed up and grumpy.*

Question: Why is not feeling fed up and grumpy important to me?
Answer: *Because I'm irritable at home and I'm not normally that sort of person.*

Question:	Why is not being irritable at home important to me?
Answer:	*Because I value my relationships and don't want to lose them.*
Final question:	What will it mean to me when I'm no longer irritable?
Answer:	*It will mean I'll be my happy self again and keep a positive relationship with my partner.*

It's worth pausing a moment here to think back to one of the foundations we explored in Chapter 3. As this exercise above will have shown, making our PhD goals matter is about seeing how they enable us to honour what we value in life. And the point is that honouring your values is a major step to motivation, enjoyment and fulfillment. Even the pathway of a PhD can be part of a fulfilling life! So it's worth remembering that goal setting is about bringing your values to life and ultimately about fulfilling that bigger picture.

At this point, then, you have an area for goal setting, you have a sense of why that is important to you and why getting it right will make a difference in your life.

What might be possible?

Taking your goal you can probably imagine some fairly predictable things that are going to follow. There will be some form of deadline that creates a limit: a final deadline for a conference abstract, or a meeting with your supervisor, university panel deadline, etc. Be it writing, reading, fieldwork, preparing for a presentation or whatever else, somehow or another, it'll happen. And part of that predictability will be about how you approach it. If it's about confidence, resilience, creativity, you might think, 'Well, yep, I know what's next: the same old, same old.'

Given you have shown you have some drive to be even doing a PhD in the first place, it's quite likely that you will do something a little bit more than that. Knowing you, you'll probably find yourself going that little bit further, even if it involves a late night, and giving that abstract a little more attention, doing a little bit more analysis, reading one more article. We all have our patterns and, let's face it: you've got to where you are now by doing what you do in the way you know best.

What, though, with a little bit of a push, might be possible? If you were at your best – motivated, organized, driven, clear – what might be possible that you could feel really proud of? What could you achieve and how would that feel?

Challenge: Finding out what's possible

Take four differently coloured cards and place them about 1 metre apart in a line on the floor. Have a fifth card to hand.

Stand at the first card and ask yourself: What is totally predictable about this goal? What is going to happen, whether I'm bored, demotivated or distracted? What will happen without putting in much effort? Write down your answer here. Notice how you feel here: how motivated are you?

Now, move to the next card along and ask yourself: What is quite probable here? What is quite likely to happen with just a little more effort, given past experience? What will I probably end up doing? Write down your answer. Again, how do you feel here?

Now, move along to the third card and ask yourself: What is possible? What am I really capable of, if I really went for it, what could happen? What might be really possible? Write down your answer here. What do you feel like in this place?

Then, moving to the fourth card and, being imaginative, now ask: What would be a completely crazy pipe dream here? What would be possible if there were no limits? Write down your answer. How does it feel here?

Finally, now go back to the first card at the start of the line and then move slowly towards the final 'pipe dream' card until you reach the point which feels right for you.

Note, there is no right place on that line. It is entirely subjective. We rarely find that PhD students stay at the predictable card, and when they do, there are usually some Gremlins lurking there saying 'can't'. Sometimes the 'probable' card feels OK. Sometimes it's between the probable and the possible, and sometimes it's between the possible and the pipe dream. And sometimes, in reviewing the other cards, PhD students realize the pipe dream isn't such a pipe dream after all . . . the pipe dream becomes what's possible.

Whether it is about a piece of writing, reading, analysis, presenting, skills, creating career opportunities, a better balance in life, feeling more confident, creative etc., this exercise should have helped you in setting a clearer vision for your goal, a clearer sense of what it is you want and can achieve.

What's possible? The draft chapter . . .

Charles was in the process of drafting final versions of his PhD chapters. He had got into a bit of a routine with his drafts, yet was feeling pretty flat. Now on his third draft chapter he was struggling to keep motivated. He had to hand it in by the end of the month to get feedback before his supervisor went away. He had got to the point where his writing had slowed right down and he was distracted by all sorts of worthy and not so worthy tasks. It was all becoming quite predictable: he'd write a few hundred words in a day that were OK, but nothing exciting. Most likely, closer to the deadline, he would do a final edit to push it along further before handing it in, knowing that it was a little half-hearted. That was fine, he'd get a PhD this way but, geez, he was getting bored. Charles reflected on his work. He realized how this had become a pattern of working and he was hungry to find some zest. He knew from his Master's dissertation what it could be like to be excited by what he was writing. Using the 'What's possible?' exercise, Charles mapped out the predictable (half-hearted writing), the probable (last-minute edit through) and identified that what was possible was to write the chapter earlier to allow a more thorough edit; the pipe dream was to complete the chapter in a way that was immediately publishable with no feedback from the supervisor. Charles pondered the 'line' from predictable to pipe dream. He realized that maybe, just maybe, the pipe dream wasn't necessarily just a pipe dream. Charles knew he had some fantastic material for each of his data chapters, and that each had something to say to a different set of literature. With more of a push and a clear sense of direction, he could in fact draft his three data chapters in the format of articles and look to submit them for publication (though still maintain the conventional thesis format). He found a space between the possible and the pipe dream that felt workable and set about drafting his chapter with more energy and excitement. He got the chapter to his supervisor on time, who of course gave him feedback, and the chapter became the basis of his first publication.

Creating a sense of progress

Knowing why our PhD goal is important and being excited by what is possible is one thing. Turning that goal into something doable is another. You probably can't get to the end result immediately – if you can, you're likely to find yourself back in the world of underwhelm. Likewise, if it's some way in the future – six months, a year, two years – then there is the risk of putting it off. Such a timeline might be underwhelming if there is no rush, or perhaps overwhelming if it's too big to think about. The bottom line here is that to make our goals more 'doable', motivating and enjoyable, we also need to be more specific about them and clearer about the steps we need to take towards them.

Note, for those of you who like to put things off, that maintaining a sense of perpetual vagueness might be just what you want. How often have we heard PhD students say, 'I'm hoping to finish around October . . . certainly by the end of the year'? We wonder how many of those students actually do finish in October. Vagueness has its advantages. It can be a safe strategy. It requires little commitment and involves considerable flexibility. Perhaps it works for you? If so, our request is for you to be curious about the payback. What do you gain from that vagueness? And what's the cost? When might a greater sense of completeness be helpful? We also invite you to try something different; you can always get the vagueness back if you want to!

How do we turn the vision of our goal into something towards which we can sense and feel progress? There is an often cited method for setting goals known as SMART. This can be represented in different ways, though the essence is to set goals that are *S*pecific, *M*easurable, *A*ttainable, *R*elevant and *T*ime-bound.

In getting to know your own motivation better, you might want to consider the following associations (our favourites) for 'ART': *A*spirational, *R*esonant and *T*hrilling.

Challenge: Smarten up your goal

Take your goal and apply the SMART formula to turn it into something that is:

1 *Specific*, i.e. clearly defined. It needs to be really clear what the goal is. The 'what's possible exercise' will have helped with that, as will

the 'what's the point?' exercise in identifying why. Here you need to get clear about the what, who, where and which of the goal.

2 *Measurable*. This could be done in different ways, e.g., in terms of time spent doing something, words written, number of contacts made, amount of data processed. This can include the total at the end, as well as what progress will look like. Here you need to be clear about how you will know when it has been completed.

3 *Attainable*. Make sure your goal is achievable. 10,000 words in one day might be a stretch too far, 1000 more likely. So this is about the 'how' of the goal and being clear about how it is going to be attainable.

4 *Relevant*. Check this is the right goal for you at this time.

5 *Time-bound*. When will the goal be completed, and what are the milestone dates?

Finally, let's put the ART into SMART:

1 How *Aspirational* is the goal for you? How much of an achievement will it be?

2 How *Resonant* is it? Does it chime with you? Is it important?

3 How *Thrilling* is it? Does the idea of achieving it excite you?

The ART of SMART . . . Monotonous tasks

Sarah had been churning away at her programming for months. It was the most boring phase of her engineering PhD, in which she had to write the program before she could do her analysis. She had become quite frustrated. There was no end in sight, it simply had to be done, and would be done when it would be done. Needless to say, she wasn't working at her best. It was as if it was getting slower and slower. Sarah was a little taken aback when her coach said, 'What's the goal here?' 'It's obvious,' she said, 'to get the programming done.' The coach prodded and Sarah began to describe what's involved in the programming, how it involved writing different sets of scripts and, prodded further, she began to identify how many scripts, how long they take her when she is working well, what sorts of things go wrong and how fantastic it would feel to have it done by January. Using the SMART formula, Sarah started to identify more specifically what was involved and what it depended on (she needed some input from a technician), identified the number of scripts that would be needed and by when each could be done. She noted, realistically, that there was a need to account for things going wrong (and she had enough experience to estimate one day in five would be about right), worked out how she could go about devising a structure to her days to make it happen, and some clear milestones along the way. As she did this, Sarah became more excited about what was possible: this had become an exciting prospect, something aspirational, resonant and thrilling!

What motivates you is what motivates you. Some PhD students want to be pushed to the edge, they want the journey to be thrilling. Others want a smoother ride, to work within their comfort zones. We are not suggesting how thrilling or aspirational your goals should be. We are suggesting that you learn what sort of goals work for you, and then ensure they are set in a way that reflects that.

We know from experience how slippery PhD students are about setting measurable time-bound goals. However, we also know that even the most intangible pieces of work, such as creative writing processes, can be more manageable and more achievable when there is a goal in sight. We all have our limits: we need sleep, food and rest. And we have deadlines. What works for you is what works for you, so be creative in exploring your goal setting. Adapting these techniques to your agenda may just make a difference . . .

Making goals smart

Example areas of PhD life	Ideas for making goals SMARTer
Writing	How many words a day, week, month? How many hours writing a day? How much time for 'free flow writing', i.e. writing to think, and how much time for 'editing', writing to present? How much time are you willing to give to it?
Reading	Numbers of articles, chapters or books read in a given time period (day, week, year) Hours spent reading Number of abstracts read Time for 'free reading' (just to stimulate the brain) Identifying the areas you want to read in.

Analysis	Number of interviews, texts, samples processed in a day Time spent each day – broken into blocks Identifying how much, each week, each month will be done
Career opportunities	Date for drafting full CV Number of networking events attended Number of contacts made, by when Number of training events attended Key skills that need to be improved
Balance in life	Time spent at work/on other things Number of times at the gym Planning specific events with friends Routine work hours and planning 'long' catch-up day
Confidence	Give a score for your confidence now (1 to 10) and identify where you would like it to be Do three tasks each day that you are putting off through lack of confidence Celebrating failing ten times a day Presenting three papers in the next six months Spot ten gremlins a day
Creativity	Spend 30 minutes every morning thinking about possibilities without any evaluation Go for a walk once a week with a note pad and scribble down any hunches Create space for 'dreaming' and work in it for one hour a day Allow free flow writing for 15 minutes in every hour of writing

Making a stretch into action . . .

There are always lots of actions that need to happen to get towards your goal. Here we want to check that, in setting your SMART goal, you've found the right place in identifying those actions between underwhelm and overwhelm. This is about finding the right degree of stretch for you.

As a warm-up for the next exercise, take a moment to do some stretching. Stand or sit and place your arms by your sides. Gently lean over to one side, as far as you comfortably can. Notice that if you leant further it could be a little painful and if you come up a little, you don't feel any stretch. Now, if you wanted to get more flexible, the challenge would be to find that place between comfort and extra stretch. This is a metaphor for thinking about stretching yourself. Everyone's stretch is different. How hard you are working is not about how far over you are leaning compared with other people, it's about the right stretch for you. So how might this relate to your PhD work?

Challenge: Taking a stretch

For this exercise, mark out on the floor ten places in a line at least six feet apart (we've sometimes found lines of trees, park benches, or gradual steps quite nice for doing this).

First, with your goal in mind, stand at the first marker and ask yourself, what is the safest possible action I could take that would move me towards my goal? Write that down under 'step 1'.

Move to the tenth marker and ask, what would be the most daring action I could take that would move me towards my goal? This should feel way beyond your comfort zone. Write that down under step 10.

Return to the first step. Ask, what would be an action that is a little less safe and involves a bit more of a stretch than the first step? Step towards the second marker and write that down.

Again, from this second marker, ask, what would be the next daring action, the next stretch? Move to the third step and write that down. Repeat this for all the intermediate steps, each becoming progressively more daring, more of a stretch, until you reach the tenth step.

Then, return to the start and take a slow walk along the markers. Settle at the step where the action feels like the right stretch for you, i.e. the best balance between safety and daring; something motivating that you will feel proud of.

Finally, what does this action mean you need to do today? No need to put it off . . .

Stretching . . . redesigning supervision

Hamza was fed up with his relationship with one of his supervisors. His supervisor had often not read the material that Hamza had sent and, when he had, was highly critical of Hamza's suggestions. Hamza was clear that he wanted considered input into his work and constructive feedback so that he knew he was making progress as he started to enter his analysis phase. He had worked through why this was important to him (why, why and why . . .?) – his growing lack of confidence was undermining the rest of his life; he was starting to feel depressed. He also explored what he felt could be possible (a constructive relationship and the possibility of an additional supervisor), and had turned this into a SMART goal (he'd identified what that constructive relationship would look like for him, how often he'd want to send material and how often he wanted to meet) and was trying to work out what his next step would be.

The first step was easy. It was more or less to do nothing (step 1). The last step, the most daring, was to immediately knock on his supervisor's door and say what he was feeling and that things had to change immediately or he would find another supervisor or consider leaving (step 10). Moving back to the first step Hamza followed through the exercise and came up with the following: send an email to his supervisor, explaining his concerns (step 2); request a meeting to explain his concerns face to face (step 3); send an email saying he wanted things to change or he'd find alternative supervision (step 4); request a meeting face to face to explain his concerns and state that things needed to change or he'd find an alternative supervisor (step 5); send an email to the departmental Post-Graduate Director and explain his concerns and the need for change (step 6); request a face-to-face meeting with the Director (step 7); send a letter to the funding body expressing his concern with supervision (step 8); knock on the Director's door now and explain the situation (step 9).

Hamza started at step 1 and realized that, since he hadn't raised this already, and because a key value for him was honesty, he would move to step 5 and be upfront with his supervisor. With the help of talking it over with a friend, he found a way of explaining his situation constructively to his supervisor. To his surprise his supervisor acknowledged that he had been distracted by the demands of a large research project and apologized. He suggested, since the work wasn't going to ease up, bringing in an additional supervisor. The three subsequently met and agreed a clear agenda for supervision meetings. Hamza also realized in the conversation that he needed to think beyond supervision for feedback and started to engage with peers and other researchers in his field.

Next steps towards your goals

Setting goals is one thing, achieving them another! While some of these exercises point you towards finding the right actions to keep you moving, it may be that you need to dig a little deeper. The other chapters in the book will help with that. Using this chapter in relation to other chapters in the book:

- Set your goals within the context of your firm foundations from Part I, and how they translate into saying 'yes' to the perfect PhD day.
- Apply goal setting to help you with getting a better balance (see Chapter 6).
- Use goal setting to help you build confidence, while using the exercises around confidence to help inform your goal setting (see Chapter 7).
- Creativity is not immune to goal setting, while bringing creativity into goal setting may help you become unstuck (see Chapter 9).
- With the right goals leading to a sense of achievement, you may feel more resilient if and when things go wrong (see Chapter 12).
- Different goals will require different kinds of support – working through the issues of relationships will be important too (see Chapter 11).
- Finally, turning goals into everyday action – that's next, how to get things done.

Actions I have taken in this chapter	✔
Chosen an area to work on	
Identified the importance to me of getting this area right (linked to my values)	
Found the place between predictable and pipe dream that works best for me	
Set a SMART goal that motivates me	
Taken steps with the right amount of stretch to turn my goal into action	
Identified which chapters of the book might be most helpful next	
Given myself a reward for doing everything on this checklist	

9

Stuck in a rut?
Being creative

Alice laughed. 'There's no use trying,' she said: 'one *can't* believe impossible things.' 'I dare say you haven't had much practice,' said the Queen. 'When I was your age, I always did it for half-an-hour a day. Why, sometimes I've believed as many as six impossible things before breakfast.'

(Lewis Carroll, *Through the Looking Glass*, 1871: 38)

'Critically discuss . . .'. Isn't that how many exam and essay questions start? It is, after all, a key skill that academic work seeks to impart, the skill of critical thinking. We learn to think critically about our subject matter, our analysis, about policy and practice, about theory. The list goes on. Perhaps it's no surprise that a retired professor who had opted out of mainstream academia said to Will some years ago, 'Get out of the university, Will, before it numbs your creativity.' And it's interesting to think that some scientists – notably James Lovelock (the Gaia theorist) and indeed Albert Einstein (no need to explain!) – found their creativity beyond the confines of academic institutions. So what about being creative when you have to be a part of a university? What happens to creativity during your PhD?

Now of course universities are full of creative people creating creative ideas in all sorts of creative processes and creative shapes and forms. And, indeed, many people are very creative in how they 'critically discuss'. Yet there are times when our critical faculties are so dominant, or indeed sometimes internalized as a form of inner critic, that we can get quite stuck in a rut. Sometimes our ideas get shot down before they have had time to fly. Think about it: when have you come across an essay or exam question that starts with the phrase, 'Creatively explore . . .'?

This chapter is about creatively exploring. It is about *being* creative. It is about finding ways to be creative at those times during your PhD when you feel 'stuck'. In a PhD you can get stuck in all sorts of ways. Perhaps you're stuck in how to work up a more exciting idea of what you could do – ways of writing about a concept or theory, say, or designing your fieldwork. Perhaps you're stuck with what to do next and how to make the PhD experience contribute to a future career. Perhaps you're stuck for motivation and need to find ways to get creative with goal setting. Or perhaps you are completely and utterly stuck in a rut, not knowing which way to turn, maybe pulling your hair out about your supervisors or how to analyse your data. Whatever the challenge, those critical faculties you have learnt through your training are probably not helping much! Whatever you are stuck with – presentations, fieldwork problems, time management, balance in life, how to deal with your supervisors, reading, writing, next steps beyond your PhD, etc. – this chapter is about findings ways to be creative; it is about creating options. After all, somewhere between being 'stuck' and believing 'impossible things' there are always options. OK, so Gremlin 'Albert' (al-but . . .) says there are not: he likes to put the big 'but' after every possible idea until it becomes a pointless option or indeed until it is exhausting trying to think about any possibilities at all (you can listen to him if you want, though we recommend a bit of time with the tools in Chapter 2 if you don't). So there are no more 'buts' in the rest of this chapter (except one at the end!). Indeed, try it now, think of a 'but', then replace it with an 'and', and feel the difference.

In this chapter we're going to offer some strategies for getting your creativity to flow, different ways to provoke your creativity, things to try out in different ways. The point is to be as creative about being creative as you can.

What will 'tapping' into your creativity more enable for you?

Where in your life will it be most valuable to have some new ideas?

Which values will you be honouring by being more creative?

In this chapter you'll find:

- ideas to give your dreamer some air time;
- suggestions for how you can create your very own playground of ideas;
- ways to create very different perspectives;
- how to let that 'Eureka' moment happen;
- lots of creative tricks and tips that PhD students have offered to get out of 'stuck' moments.

Giving your dreamer some playtime

Walt Disney is a helpful starting point for being creative in your PhD. He recognized the problems of being stuck and the need to be creative. He noticed how too much critique and judgement could stifle the creative process, even if well intentioned. Disney's solution was simple. He separated out the processes of dreaming (imagine what if . . .), of being a realist (how could that work . . .) and being a critic (why would we . . .). Literally he created different rooms to be in for these different processes and those rooms had quite different characteristics and layouts. As his business grew, he apparently put his dreamers, his creative people, in a separate building from those who needed a more critical or more practical eye (the accountants, technicians and marketing people). What can we learn from Disney for being creative in the PhD, for getting out of a rut, or even just to be able to open up more possibilities?

Our suggestion is quite simple. You have to suspend your critical faculties and create some time to become more creative. How to do that?

In Chapter 2 we've already suggested quite a few techniques for putting down your critical voices when they emerge in the name of Gremlins ('but', 'no way', 'you can't', 'don't risk it', etc.). Gremlins will not help you be creative. There are other critical voices that are important, though, and these come in a more evaluative form – perhaps examining the practicalities of an idea or whether indeed the idea really does meet the criteria of what you are looking for. In the moment of being creative, these too – though useful in other stages – need to be quiet. To really allow your creative juices to flow, it's also important to put aside any critical voices that are likely to inhibit free flowing thinking. So our first step is about suspending those critical voices until the time when they are required.

Don't worry. Dreaming is just dreaming, none of these dreams are going to happen if you don't want them to. And after you have finished your dreaming, you can bring back those critical voices in the ways you want to, to allow some evaluation to work out exactly what the best options are for you. That part of the process is not for here. You'll find more on moving from your dreams to reality in Chapters 8 and 10 which deal with turning thoughts into action. Here, we just want you to dream . . .

Challenge: Creating playtime!

Like the Queen in *Through the Looking Glass*, it's worth allowing some space to dream the impossible. Planning time to be creative may sound dull and even ironic. Knowing we have time to dream, to play, makes all the difference though. It means you can be free to dream, knowing that there will be time to evaluate, because you've planned for this. This might be about planning how you manage a few hours. For example, if you have 2 hours set aside to write an abstract, perhaps spend 20 minutes of 'playtime' at the start to see what comes out. Or it might be about how you conduct a meeting: perhaps for a 1-hour meeting to discuss the next possibilities for your fieldwork, you set aside 15 minutes to creatively explore the possibilities, suspending any evaluation during that process. Or it may be that in the process of writing a literature review, you plan to allow one day for free flow thinking about the many different ways you could put it together and how ideas link, before evaluating the best options for you. And it might be that, like the Queen in *Through the Looking Glass*, you build into your routine time to think the impossible, as a matter of habit. What could you try that might work for you? Set a goal here to 'give your dreamer some air time'. When and how might this happen? What will you commit to trying for the next week? Be playful! What could you start today . . .?

A small detour on dreaming: At a workshop when we introduced these ideas to some PhD students, one student said, quite fairly, 'What's the point of thinking of impossible things, of creating loads of ideas that, well, we already know quite frankly are not realistic?' Fair point. An important point. Our response was threefold (we were feeling creative!). The first is something we brought up in Part I of this book about thinking big. Many apparently impossible ideas have, in due course, happened (landing on the moon, the end of apartheid in South Africa, the four-minute mile, etc.). There is some value in thinking the impossible. Second, if we want to stop a process of creating new ideas, there is no better way than to start evaluating each one as it comes up. Try it out. Before long you won't even speak an idea because all the problems will have arisen before it gets uttered. Third, there is a lot to be learnt about what's possible from what is impossible. The 'impossible' – out there, curve ball, lateral thinking, off-centre – may just have something in it, a kernel of something that may lead to other options and ultimately to the solution you are looking for. And fourth (we are more creative than we realized!), often the best ideas come from combinations of different ideas, so letting all the ideas get 'out there' might allow new combinations to form that will hit the nail on the head. Two wrongs don't make a right, two impossibles might!

Letting go of the writing critic

Writing can be a painful and slow process, and at worst we can get completely stuck – the infamous 'writing block'. Jon was in his third year and had a writing block (sounds like an illness when said that way). He followed all the advice on how to write: he had a regular time in the day in which he wrote, he created a special space for writing, he would take regular breaks. He knew the conditions for him that were good for writing. And he knew he could write well; he'd had some great feedback in the past. Something had changed, though. Jon was feeling the pressure to perform. While previously he had been writing work for discussion – 'drafts', we might say – now it was time to produce the real thing, his final PhD. So, despite hours at the computer, there wasn't much to show for it except many half-written sentences moving down the pages as he tried to find the right way to start.

Jon was stuck. Remembering back to when he wrote well, Jon realized that he wrote at his best when he was in an exploration mode, a mode when he wasn't so worried about 'presenting' to the reader. It was more of a mode of 'writing to think' rather than writing down what he had thought. How could he recreate that now when so much was at stake? Jon did some work on quietening down his Gremlins, and then got creative. He played a little trick on himself by deciding to separate out his writing into two processes: first, he would allow himself to write to 'think', and then he would focus on editing his writing to 'present'. That wasn't easy at first so Jon played and added a few additional tricks: in the first mode, he *changed the font to a more friendly one*, eg Chalkboard and wore relaxed clothes, while in the second mode, he'd *change the font to something formal* eg Times New Roman and put on a shirt!

Let your dreamer have a playground

Giving your dreamer some time to play is one thing. Where, though, are you at your most creative? How to create a space, a place, where you can be really creative? – that's the challenge here.

How often have you heard someone say, 'I was really stuck, so I sat at my desk and thought really, really hard while staring at the screen, and suddenly it came to me!' OK, so you might be in a more imaginative space at the desk, surfing the internet to take you somewhere else. Fair enough if that works for you. There is the risk, though, in the words of Eliza Dolittle (a pop singer) in her song 'Pack up', 'When I Google I only get depressed . . .'.

More often you hear people say things like, 'It was weird, I was in the supermarket and saw the bread being stacked up and I realized. . . .'. Or, 'I was cycling home last night and it suddenly dawned on me that . . .'. In the supermarket, on your bike, on the golf course, talking a walk, lying awake at 2.00 a.m., watching a film, etc. – these kinds of situations are so often when the ideas that count often emerge. How to create a playful space for ideas to emerge?

Challenge: Create your PhD playground

For this to work, you have to do it, not just think about doing it. So give this a go and enjoy the results.

The ingredients for your PhD playground:

- a place with plenty of space that allows movement (inside or outside, wherever is good for you);
- some random objects around the place (perhaps toys, food, bags, things already there);
- music or sounds (try out different kinds);
- different coloured paper and colourful pens spread about;

- willingness to do things differently.

Instructions:

- wash off any Gremlins (or write them down and place them in a bin in the corner) and replace with a childlike playfulness;
- suspend any evaluation criteria, you can bring them in at some other time and place;
- give yourself permission to try out a different way of working;
- move about that space (perhaps stand on one leg, jump about, forward roll!);
- use the paper and pens to write and draw ideas and move them about;
- be silly, be visual, be audio, be . . .

You've allocated some playtime, you've created a playground place. What else?

Creating playful perspectives

It's all a matter of perspective. Is your glass half-full or half-empty – and do you even care? All are different perspectives on the same thing. The power of adopting different perspectives is something that can be used during your PhD in all sorts of ways.

You might say, well, that's part of being able to be critical: being able to critically explore different perspectives. That can be a creative exercise. Think, for example, of how we might read a really difficult bit of material. We can do it in so many different ways. We might read it from a point of view of analysing its logical coherence, perhaps asking whether the conclusions follow from the findings (or, for philosophers, if the conclusions follow from premises). We might also read it from the point of view of empirical reality: does what we are reading match up to what we know about the world? We might read it from the point of view of how it is written: is it clear, concise, are there too many long words, or is it too straightforward, not elaborate enough, too simplistic? Sure, these are all valid and important ways to read a text. There are more, though. Imagine reading a piece of poetry with the perspectives outlined above. How different might that feel compared with allowing the poetry to take you into another way of seeing the world, or indeed into another way of being with the world? Where do these words take me? How do they impact on me? What do they allow me to see? How do they encourage me to be? What doors might they open up?

Clearly, taking a different perspective is not only about being in your head. Different perspectives can create very different emotional states within which very different ideas might emerge.

Challenge: Playful perspectives

You can use different perspectives as a way to help you tap into your creativity. We might call it something like 'provoking insights from random association' or a 'perspective generator'. We're not going to call it that, though. We're going to call the tool here 'pizza slices'. Note, you might want to call it something else, especially if you're being creative and don't like pizza. It goes like this . . .

1 In your playground, imagine you have a huge pizza on the floor (you can use it elsewhere too if you want, it's a take-away pizza!). You might want to mark it out with tape or place some different bits of cards in different places. In the middle of the pizza is the thing you want to be creative about ('writing', 'jobs', 'supervision' etc.).
2 Each 'slice' has different toppings. We've provided some toppings for you to try below, and you can create many more. A top tip: keep it as playful as possible because this is about 'dreaming', not evaluating. And keep some variety – it is after all the spice of life!
3 Go and have a taste of each one. Really get into the place of each slice. That might mean looking away from the centre and finding out what that place says to you. For example, think about someone who is a hero. When you think of them, what do you see? What do you hear? What do you feel? And then look back at the centre. What does that perspective allow you to see? What possibilities, however random, emerge? Write these down or draw on separate Post-it notes or cards. Let each idea or variation of an idea have its very own note or card. Once you're done with ideas in one place free your mind of that perspective and move to the next.

Here's an example of some perspectives you might choose.

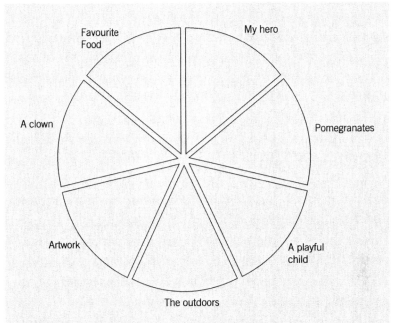

Creative Perspectives

4   Are there others slices you want to add in? Any random connections in the space that may provoke something? Look out of the window perhaps. Is there some air-conditioning? A fire extinguisher? Chair, table? Put them upside down, and what do you see? What other options or ideas do they generate?

Other perspectives to try on

Favourite film	Best holiday	A sport
Laughter	Cartoon character	Spaceman
A monk	Leisure	A garden plant
A drink	An animal	A poet

5   Bring all your ideas into one place. Look across the ideas, play with the connections between them and see what else emerges.

Perhaps some really clear options are opening up for you? Now you may want to take those ideas and move to another place – and some other time – to evaluate them?

Thinking creatively about your supervisors

How often someone is 'stuck' because of a poor relationship with their supervisors. For Julia, it felt like there were no options. She felt she had to accept she couldn't have a constructive relationship with her supervisors, that they would always act superior to her, that they would always put her ideas down. She had told herself just to put her head down and get on with things. Julia reached a point where her morale was so low and her self-esteem so poor that she was close to giving up. Having ruled out the possibility of changing supervisors – no-one else in her department knew the field – Julia decided it was time to get creative.

Julia went for a walk in some nearby woods and found a space where there was a small clearing. In it she imagined a 'pizza' with six different slices. On them she put 'When everything was just so', 'Tomatoes', 'My best ever holiday', 'My favourite film star', 'Skydiving', 'Trees' (since one was there!). Spending time in each one Julia started to create all sorts of options of what she could do about supervision. Here's how it went:

- 'When everything was just so' related to her time as an undergrad student when she'd have fascinating discussions with friends in the coffee bar: could she ask to have supervision in coffee bars?
- 'Tomatoes' reminded her of fresh salad: could she let go of her assumptions of their supervision meetings and approach them with a fresh state of mind?
- 'My best ever holiday' was one in which she had lots of friends with different interests doing different things: could she think of a wider group of people she could rely on for feedback and not just her supervisors?
- 'My favourite film star' turned out to be Ben Kingsley playing Gandhi, which made her think about breaking down hierarchy: what would supervision look like if she assumed there wasn't a hierarchy, if they were partners? How differently would she act?
- 'Skydiving' was something Julia always wanted to do and was scared of: what if she stopped treating supervision as a scary adventure and instead saw it as exhilarating to confront? Could she be brave enough to raise the issue with them?
- From a 'Trees' perspective Julia saw something strong, steady and deep-rooted. Supervision suddenly seemed a relatively light issue in the bigger scheme of life.

Julia wrote down each of these questions and ideas and put some time aside the next day to come up with a strategy. She decided she wanted to be brave and to confront the situation with a real conversation about how she felt ('Film star' plus 'Skydiving') and see if they could create a fresh way of working ('Tomatoes'). However, she would do this with a sense of lightness ('Trees') and while also engaging with other peers to talk about her and their work over coffee ('Holiday' plus 'just so').

Allowing that 'Eureka!' moment to happen

Insight is not a light bulb that goes off inside our heads. It is a flickering candle that can easily be snuffed out.
(Malcolm Gladwell, *Blink: The Power of Thinking Without Thinking*. New York: Little, Brown, 2005: 122)

Sometimes we just know. We have a gut feeling. We have an idea that feels just right. It may even jump out at us. Eureka is an ancient Greek word meaning, literally, 'I've found it'. It's a moment of sudden and unexpected discovery. Archimedes is said to have had his Eureka moment in the bath. Perhaps you have had one in the past (a Eureka moment, not a bath)? Perhaps you've had one during your PhD? In the description of Eureka above, the words 'sudden' and 'unexpected' are significant. It's as if the 'thought' came spontaneously from somewhere else and just popped through the letter box and into our heads without warning. And, of course, our intuition 'speaks' in all sorts of ways: body language, dreams, emotions, hunches, gut feelings. It can be hard to put into words ('it just feels wrong'), can be difficult to trust, can appear irrational, illogical, spooky, off the wall, even! And yet, it can be the very source of the creative inspiration we need. The question is: can we encourage such moments to jump out? Creating the time and space for some creative thinking could be a good start. And trying on different perspectives may also help. What more can we do to foster being in touch with our intuition?

Challenge: Set your intuition free

So our intuition is bubbling away below the surface just waiting to be set free. Some examples of where this could be particularly valuable are in decision-making, when brainstorming ideas, during problem solving and any situation requiring a quick response. Here are three ways you can encourage your intuition to surface more freely.

- *Blurting.* Say the first thing that comes to mind no matter how ridiculous it seems. OK, so it might be 'off the mark' but you'll never know until you let it out and have the chance to consider it.
- *Metaphor.* Intuition is sensed in non-verbal ways which is one reason it can seem tricky to articulate. Try expressing whatever you are thinking by using images and metaphors that pop into your mind. For example 'As I thought of that it was like snowflakes landing on a roof' or 'That idea feels like a runaway train about to come off the track' or 'The answer seems to be like a bowl of fruit.'
- *Gut feeling.* Tune into your body and literally say what you are feeling at that moment. For example 'I feel all hot and prickly when I think about it that way', or 'Hearing that idea makes my stomach churn' or 'My tummy tingles at the thought of going down that road.' Over time you will discover more about what these sensations are telling you and learn to trust your 'gut feeling'.

Intuitive responses can often seem strange when first expressed, however, by practising letting them free you will considerably increase your chances of more 'Eureka moments'. Now set yourself a goal for the next week to try one or more of the above as often as you can.

And some tips and tricks

Following the ideas in this chapter and taking the challenges will get your creativity going. To add to the possibilities of possibilities, we've come across all sorts of creative solutions to what can appear 'typical' PhD problems and we thought it only fair to share them with you. That's what we do here.

Tips and tricks for being creative with your writing . . .

- Try imagining you are writing a letter: 'Dear Uncle Jim, did you know that the PhD experience doesn't have to be so miserable? Let me tell you more about how people can get more out of it. First, I'll tell you about foundations, then I'll tell you . . .' etc.
- Try different fonts. Some fonts feel very serious and maybe you need that (sometimes it helps me take the writing more seriously). Some fonts are more playful and make me loosen up a little. And some fonts are very neat and tidy, sometimes I need that. So try different fonts to see what happens to your writing and to how you feel.
- Try adding some colour. Perhaps try changing the background colour of the page, or changing the colour of the font. Again, notice what happens . . . Maybe change it every 20 minutes or so (a change is as good as a break, they say!)
- Try working somewhere else. If you can, a different table, a different angle, a different room. A café, bar, library, office, home, dining table, etc. Lots of choices!
- Try working offline. Pen and paper. Coloured pens and coloured paper.
- And try, why not, different ways of writing? Try planning what you are writing more. Try planning what you are writing less.
- Music, coffee, water, juice? Whatever your fix. More of? Less of?
- Build in rewards . . . for words, for time spent . . .
- Try a regular slot for writing. A few hundred words a day keeps the supervisor away!
- Turn writing into talking, record it and then transcribe.
- If you are really, really, really stuck . . . try writing about why you are stuck.
- Remember: when drafting, deleting it all is an option! So write what you want, evaluate later.
- Try laying out the 'draft' on the floor in front of you. You'll see it differently. You'll see the relationship between ideas in new ways. See which bits are long, which bits are short. Use colours to mark them, connect them up.
- Imagine a friendly audience – what do you need to tell them to help them learn about what you want to say?

Tips and tricks for being creative with reading . . .

- Where are you reading? Same desk that you write at and check emails? Where else might you try reading? Does noise work for you (how many times does your supervisor say 'I'll read your draft on the train back where there are no distractions'?)

- What posture works for you? Relaxed, perhaps in an armchair? More upright, more focused in an office chair? How does that shift your relationship to what you are reading?
- The atmosphere. Does music, radio or silence work for you? Certain smells (oil burner, joss sticks, coffee?). What fix, if any, works for you – coffee (decaf always an option!), green tea, juice, water?
- What format are you reading? On screen – what size font, what colour background? On paper?
- Making notes? How do you do that? Hand-written, computer? While you are reading or afterwards (e.g. spend 15 minutes writing down what you learnt from the article)?
- What attitude helps you read? Do you need to be fascinated, intrigued, puzzled, pressured, scared, perplexed?
- How long do you want to spend on it? Will asked a professor of sociology how long he would spend on a book and he said no more than two hours. A whole book! He said you can get the argument and focus on interesting bits in that time and always go back for more if you need to.
- Linking reading to writing. How would it work for you to consolidate what you've read with some exploratory writing (not just note taking)? Note: not writing to present but writing to explore!
- Back to basics (because we often forget). Try methods like SQ3R (survey, question, read, recite and review) or various 'speed' reading books.

Tips and tricks for bring creative about supervision

- What different conversations could you create with your supervisors that you are not having now?
- What different assumptions about your supervisors could you try adopting?
- When do you defer to their expertise when you might in fact be in a better place to make a decision? When could you tell them what is needed?
- What if your supervisors are acting from a place of lack – a lack of confidence, time, creativity? If you rely on them, and they produce from a place of lack, what does that mean for your PhD and your confidence?
- What do you expect from your supervisors? In mapping out what you are expecting from your supervisors, is it possible to 'fill up' some of that from other people (including yourself)?

- A bigger team? Thinking about all the different things supervisors can do, who else can contribute to that? Who else might read and comment on some of your work? Who else can advise on next steps, on how to overcome problems? Who else can you talk to about the intellectual ideas contained in your project? Who else can you share ideas with about innovative fieldwork or the struggles of getting it done? Who else can recommend key reading? Who else can . . .?; the list is endless here. And so too is the list of people . . . other staff, other peers in your department, peers in other departments, peers and staff at other UK universities, at global universities. Your research team could span the world!!! Indeed, if you were to pick the perfect players in your PhD team, who would they be and what tasks would they perform?
- Do you know that feeling of meeting in an academic office when the supervisor has one eye on his email and one eye watching you (sort of!)? There are options here for changing that dynamic. Where do you meet? How do you all sit? How do you communicate (email, phone, in the corridor)? And what might it be helpful to notice in supervision? What do you do? How do you sit? How do you talk? What are you feeling when you talk? What do you listen to? What do you make notes on? How would you like to feel? What would you like to look like, sit like, talk like if it was going swimmingly well? What would happen if any of these things changed?
- How might you conduct the meetings differently? Check out ways to conduct professional meetings (aims and goals of the meeting, brief reminder of where things were at last time, clarify how much time is available and where you'd like to get to, what your expectations of the meeting are . . .).
- Your writing – do you present it on time? How professional does it look? Via email, hard copy?

Next steps to being creative

Being creative is about letting ideas flow freely without any of the 'buts' jumping in. That requires separating out the time for being creative from the time for other forms of thinking where critical skills might be helpful. It can also help to separate out the place for doing creative thinking. And it can help to follow the Queen's advice from *Through the Looking Glass*, to allow the impossible some air time and see where it takes you. Within all of that, your intuition might be allowed to speak and have just the answers you are looking for. It's one thing to read about these ideas; what about now putting them into practice?

Actions I have taken in this chapter	✔
Taken time each day to think creatively ('dreamer')	
Used my creative environment ('playground') when I want to be more creative	
Generated some new options/ideas by using playful perspectives ('pizza')	
Practised listening to and acting on my intuition ('Eureka!')	
Tried out at least two of the tips and tricks	
Become more aware of 'buts' in my language and replaced some with 'and'	
Given myself a creative reward for doing everything on this checklist	

10

Distracted?

Giving yourself permission to re-find your focus

When your mind isn't clouded by unnecessary things,
This is the best season of your life.
(Wu-Med, quoted by Jon Kabat-Zinn, *Wherever You Go,
There You Are*. London: Piatkus, 2004: 16)

There are so many distractions from the PhD. Perhaps you get distracted by your own curiosity – wanting to find out more, to read that little bit extra? Perhaps your distraction comes in the shape of anxiety about the future, putting your energy into things you want to have in place to secure a job? Perhaps your distractions come in the form of daydreams, thinking about the weekend, your lover, holiday plans? Maybe you have habits that distract you: email, Facebook, Twitter, the news, surfing the web? Perhaps it's other people interrupting? Or you find yourself overwhelmed by the many things that need doing, so you jump from one thing to the next like a plate spinner? Perhaps you distract yourself with self-doubt? With food, or coffee. Maybe your distraction serves as a general state of procrastination that, well, keeps you putting things off? And so on . . . We doubt this list is anywhere near complete. We could get distracted thinking of yet more . . .!

Be distracted no more! This chapter is about getting focused, being present to get the PhD work you need to do done. Two words are really important: being and doing. We need both here. Without being focused we find ourselves drifting, disconnected from where we are and unsure as to whether we are making progress. Yet through doing things we can sometimes find that state of being focused. Being and doing can work together here. This chapter is about things we can do to get focused and at the same time it is about finding a way to keep being focused. It is about being in a way that gives you permission to focus on the present!

How often do you let yourself down by not doing what you say you will?

What will it mean to you to be more consistent in what you do?

Who are you being when you get distracted from what's important?

In this chapter you will be able to give yourself permission to do the following:

- review your distractions and discover what being focused is like for you;
- get focused with help from some backward planning;
- put first things first and prioritize your day;
- manage interferences and get done what you want to get done;
- 'bust' the procrastination habit and move forwards.

A short, not too distracting, review

Being distracted: whether it's by email, coffee, holidays, weather, noise or whatever is a way of being. Watching the close-ups in the Olympics at the time of writing shows only too well how the athletes in their various sports spend time getting into the right 'state of mind' to be able to focus on their competition. This takes us right back to the start of this book and the possibility that we can create shifts in perspective and that such shifts can bring about a different way of approaching things, a different way of being.

Before we go further, then, to really check with the 'being' part of your distractions, below are some questions to answer which may mean you need to go back to other parts of the book first. What is missing that means the reward for focus is just not enough, or indeed feels too much, to be able to take the risk? What is the cost of not being focused, and what is the pay-off? If these are difficult questions to answer, then some of the previous chapters are going to provide some crucial foundations to re-finding your focus and getting things done.

Challenge: A short, not too distracting, review

- Are you distracted by a Gremlin that is provoking self-limiting beliefs? It could be very well disguised, coming in the form of telling you about all the other important things that need doing first. Or it might be very explicit: 'What's the point? It's not going to work.' It could be saying all sorts of things. The important thing here is that if Gremlins are present, they will hold you back from focusing. In which case, return to Chapter 2 to employ some Gremlin-busting tricks! That may also require re-finding your confidence, in which case Chapter 7 is also important.
- Are you distracted by a lack of clarity as to why you are doing a PhD, i.e., what you value about doing the PhD? If that is the case, you may need to remind yourself what is it about being focused that you value (see Chapters 3 and 4 on Finding value in your PhD and Tapping into your bigger picture).
- Is your distraction emerging from a sense of being generally out of balance, feeling like things have got out of control? If this feels the case, then it is worth reviewing Chapter 6 to find a better balance.
- Do you find yourself unsure as to what exactly the aim is at this point, what your goals are, what you need to achieve? Are you unsure of whether you are making any progress? If so, then working out what your goals are will be a good start (see Chapter 8).
- Finally, your distractions may be so strong at this point that you need to rekindle a sense of resilience, to feel in a good place to approach the demands of the PhD. You may be experiencing a sense of 'burnout' and exhaustion. As well as building on all of Part I, Chapter 12 could be important here.

If you have reviewed the questions above and addressed any issues relevant to you, then at this point you will be clear about needing to find some practical ways to re-find your focus, and that is the focus of the rest of this chapter.

Before we jump into the detail, though, there are just a few more questions to reflect on:

- Why is it important to get your focus? Is it about your PhD? Your sanity? Sense of fulfilment? Enjoyment of each moment? We all have different answers to this: what for you is important about finding your focus?
- How do you know when you are focused? What does it feel like? What state of mind are you in? What do people around you notice?

Beyond techniques

Jenny was an English PhD student who found herself very busy. She was doing all sorts of exciting things that engaged her with her peers, with research groups as well as with other activities through sport. Although Jenny was excited by everything she was involved in, she often found herself so busy doing this, that and the other that some of her core PhD work kept slipping behind. All was going well until a review panel at the end of her second year in which the academics questioned whether she should have developed some of her writing much more, given the stage she was at. At first, Jenny tried to look at various techniques for managing time, for prioritizing tasks. They all seemed straightforward enough, yet when she applied them, things would still slip. In other words, things did slip! Jenny took a step back. She realized she needed to look more fundamentally at what was important to her and what was at stake in not moving forward. Having tapped more into her values, that rekindled what was important to her about her writing and getting on with the PhD. She also realized that she had some Gremlins that were provoking some self-doubt which made it easier to put things off than to dare to confront them. With a clearer sense of her values, and having brought her Gremlins under control, the techniques for time management and goal setting became more relevant and started to work.

Permission to focus: some backward planning

Long gone are the days (if they ever existed) when the boundaries of a PhD were undefined: what it involved was whatever it involved, and it was a mystery to the uninitiated! In those days, or at least in that caricature, the PhD student had permission to follow their nose; they had little time pressure and no word limits and could explore whatever they felt was important. They had permission to focus on what they wanted to, without the pressures many students feel today to produce results. Indeed, some of you reading this may similarly read what you need to read when you want to read it, dwelling upon ideas and writing things down when inspiration takes hold or designing new and more exciting versions of experiments just to see where it takes you.

For the majority of PhD students, however, there seems to be more pressure than that. Pressures from the institution to finish within a certain time frame, pressures from yourself to finish within an affordable time frame, pressures on making sure you are doing the right things for future employment, pressures to generate your argument in fewer words. All in all, while three or four years can feel like a long time at the start, quite quickly there can be a lot of tasks to do and it can feel like there is not enough time to coordinate them. You can find yourself 'plate spinning' – running from one thing to the next, trying to keep everything going, and anxious in case anything slips.

Time and time again when coaching PhD students who are stressed and distracted by the challenge of plate spinning, we find that, when pushed a little to describe more about the tasks at hand, they reveal that while the goal appears to be very clear, the detail of what's involved is missing. No wonder it can become stressful and feel like a very long and complicated 'to do' list with no clear end in sight. They get distracted by jumping from one thing to the next. They don't give themselves permission to be focused.

One way to give yourself permission to focus on the task at hand is to be clear that what you are focusing on needs doing now, and that there is a time and a place for the other tasks elsewhere in your schedule. Indeed, having a schedule of what needs doing by when in order to enable other things to happen could be the key word here. In other words, a plan! Now, plans start with a goal in mind, so, we're assuming here that this is the case (please review Chapter 8 to ensure this is so!). With the goal – the endpoint – in mind, it's a case of backward planning by mapping out in detail what needs doing and by when in order to get to where you want to be. A neat way to do this is with a Gantt chart that places different tasks alongside each other in a way that you can coordinate what needs doing by when. This enables you to focus on one task without worrying about how there will be time to do everything else. It gives you permission to be present to the task at hand.

Challenge: Your permission to focus chart

Here's a way to build your 'permission to focus' Gantt chart. Start with your clear goal in mind:

- First, list all the tasks that you need to complete in order to achieve the goal. Write down any other things that need to happen to complete those tasks. You now have a list of all the tasks that need doing.
- Then, estimate how much time each task will take. Note some tasks will be really clear, e.g. one hour, and some will be vaguer, e.g. two or three days.
- Now, create a rough chart based on the example below. Do it roughly because you'll want to be able to chop and change to get it right. Spreadsheets are one way to do this. If you are not sure what a Gantt chart is or how to create one, there are many resources on the internet. The following link is an example of one: http://office.microsoft.com/en-001/excel-help/create-a-gantt-chart-in-excel-HA001034605.aspx.
- Once you have a rough chart that appears to work, check that you have built in some room for slack, i.e., room for things to slip or go wrong – a buffer zone. Use your experience to gauge how much slack you may need.
- Create a neater version that you can use to assess where you are up to and what needs adjusting as time moves on. Gantt charts have the benefit of making clear the 'critical path' of a project.

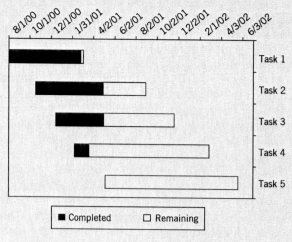

Gantt Chart

Some things to note in your giving-yourself-permission to focus chart:

- What level of detail do you need in order to be able to focus? You need to experiment and find out what works for you. Generally, if the chart is for a larger task that takes you some time into the future, the level of detail will be less, since it's hard to know that far in advance for many PhDs exactly what will be required and by when. The shorter the timescale, the more detail is possible. So it might be, for example, you find it helpful to have a general chart (say, the whole PhD) in which you map out different phases or chapters, a three-month chart (perhaps for a period of writing or fieldwork) in which the level of detail is in terms of weekly goals, and then perhaps a chart over a couple of weeks with daily detail.
- While there is no right or wrong way to create your chart, one thing is for sure: things don't always happen how we want them to. It's important therefore to build in your 'buffer zone' in a way that works for you. For some it might be that for every six weeks' work, you plan a 'spare' week; for others it may be adding one day in every four. How wonderful if all goes well and you have more time to play with! It's also important to build in reviews in which you assess where you are and whether the next stages need adjusting.

Permission to focus, building in some slack

John was a third year IT student and was struggling to write. The chapter that faced him seemed like one huge amorphous bundle, and he simply could not seem to make any progress. John explored setting some goals for when this chapter would be done. He spoke to some peers who were close to submission and they said that's just how it is: 'just keep going'. Not satisfied by the weighty feeling of the ongoing burden of there being an unknown end to the task, John wanted to explore how he might set some goals for his chapter that would help him know he was doing the right thing each day. John tried to set up a Gantt chart. However, it didn't feel right. How could he possibly plan his writing? What if he got to bits that are much harder than he expected, what about all the interruptions that might get in his way, what about if he simply can't get in the mood to write and it takes much longer? What if, what if, what if . . .?

John's coach challenged him: given John has been writing for some years now (degree, Master's, PhD), doesn't he actually have quite a good sense of how long it takes to do things? And doesn't he also have a good sense of how much time can slip? And so can't John build that into his plan? In reflecting on that, John worked out that, for him, planning three days of 'slack' for every ten days of writing was probably about right. He re-made his plan for the chapter to be finished in six weeks, and then created a detailed plan for the first two weeks. To his surprise, he finished his first two weeks' tasks ahead of schedule. Having used the plan to give himself permission to focus each day, he'd actually found a new way of writing that was more effective than before.

Permission to put first things first

Things which matter most
Must never be at the mercy of things which matter least.
(Goethe, cited by Stephen Covey, *The 7 Habits of Highly Effective People: Restoring the Character Ethic*.
New York: Simon & Schuster, 1989: 146)

There is so much to be done in a PhD. Aren't 'to do' lists just great? Do you ever find yourself writing them as a way of avoiding what's in front of you? Do you find that, as you write a 'to do' list, you can identify what feels like lots of quick hits that make you feel you are getting things done, like you are keeping busy? Or do you have a Gremlin that is so worried about everything you have to do, it is constantly getting you to write lists? We want you to let go of the 'to do' list habit for the moment, and think instead of giving yourself permission to put first things first.

The common mistake often made with 'to do' lists is to forget to think about what's most important. Following a 'to do' scheme can involve conflating urgency with importance and with priority. 'To do' lists tend to have what appear to be the most urgent tasks at the top, as the priority, with other highly important tasks that are for the future somewhere near the bottom. How often do you spend the first part of your day 'clearing' your 'to do' list with a promise to do some reading, writing, or analysis in the afternoon, only to find by then that either more 'to dos' have appeared or you're too drained to focus?

Focusing on urgent tasks as a priority also means that you often don't quite get to what matters. One academic colleague once said: 'For the past ten years I've always assumed that in two weeks I will have cleared all the bits and pieces and be able to get on with my writing. It has never happened yet.' Of course, in time the future tasks become urgent and perhaps you find yourself writing to the last-minute deadline, submitting an abstract right at the last second, cramming your analysis, and so on. It's an all-too-common experience, and one that is stress-provoking.

So what might be an alternative? How might you organize your PhD work in a way that means you give yourself permission to get on with the important things? The challenge each day is to put first things first, where first things are the important things. If your house is on fire, do you finish doing the dishes first or get out of the house?

Challenge: The 'first things first' daily planner

- First, using a table like the one below, jot down in column 1 all the things you want to achieve today: the results of today's work.
- Identify how much time you want to give to achieving each of those results. How long are you willing to give? (See the last column.)
- Look at your list and decide on relative importance, scoring 1 for most important, 2 for less important, and so on. Note, commit to 1, 2, 3, 4, etc. – don't let two things be scored as '1'!
- Rank for urgency, giving A for most urgent, B for less urgent, and so on.
- Make a decision, based on the balance of urgency and importance, about what order to do things in. Play to your strengths. When are you at your best to perform the tasks that need the most of you?
- Once you have your priorities in a well-considered order, you can write them straight into your diary or planner and do away with your 'to do' list habit altogether!

First things first

Results to achieve	Importance rating 1,2,3, etc.	Urgency ranking A,B,C, etc.	Order in which to action 1st, 2nd, 3rd etc.	Time required, e.g. 30 minutes, 2 hours, etc.

Note: be curious about when it is best for you to devise your daily plan. For example, if you are a bit of a worrier and find it hard to switch off, there are advantages to planning for the next day at the end of the previous one and committing your plan to paper. It's a way of emptying your mind of all the things you have to do so that you can enjoy your rest time without fussing or worrying about the next day. Alternatively, some people prefer to do it at the start of the day, and then review it at the end to feel a sense of satisfaction.

Making the day how you want it to be

Rhea had a mountain of biological analysis to do. It was the sort of PhD that would involve months of mundane, repetitive processing of samples before she could get anywhere near doing the analysis and know what her results might be. Rhea had become anxious about being in touch with her subject. She was getting to know more about Radio 1 music (one way to make the processing more fun) than she was about her subject. Rhea had decided to set herself some reading targets to keep in touch with the research debates. However, each day she found that all sorts of 'priorities' would emerge that meant she didn't get her lab work started until late in the morning and then, to keep up, would be doing that through to early evening. By the end of the day she was too exhausted to read anything. Over time Rhea found that her days were structured around ticking off jobs from her 'to do' list before getting into her analysis. Reflecting on how she'd confused doing 'urgent' things with the 'priorities', she realized that not only was her lab work slipping, so too was her reading. Rhea spent some time re-thinking her daily plans and developed a new structure to the day. She shifted things around, reading a paper first thing in the day, then doing some lab processes until 30 minutes before lunch. In that 30 minutes she would check her emails and transfer emails to jobs (rather than let the inbox be a 'to do' list). In the afternoon she'd do more processing and then plan in some time for other tasks that she wanted to get done. Last thing in the afternoon she'd find the article to read for the next day and have that ready to read the next morning. By moving the reading to the start of the day, Rhea found herself reflecting on the research during the lab processing and felt generally more motivated and content with her research.

Permission to manage interferences (and to get done what you want to get done)

All living things contain a measure of madness that moves them in strange, sometimes inexplicable ways. This madness can be saving; it is part and parcel of the ability to adapt. Without it, no species would survive.

(Yann Martel, *Life of Pi*, London: Canongate Books, 2003: 52)

Plans are great, but they don't always work out as you intended. Even the best daily plan may go wrong. That's fine, because in our overall planning we've built in some space for that – a buffer zone. However, plans also go wrong because of general interferences: things that get in the way, things that we let get in our way and which, over time, mean the things that matter don't get done.

Interferences come in all sorts of shapes and forms. Sometimes they appear as unavoidable interruptions, as must do's, as things that emerge that need urgent attention, such as requests from supervisors. Sometimes they come in the form of things going wrong: perhaps the computer gets a virus, perhaps you get a virus, you get stuck in a traffic jam, or suchlike. And sometimes they come as nice temptations: a call from an old friend, some good news, and so on. Whether we like them or not, though, they are 'interferences' if they push us off track from what we want to be doing. It might be that they need your attention, and if that's the case, it's your choice to devote time to them. How aware are you of how you are managing your interferences? How often do you get distracted by interferences you could avoid?

Challenge: Spotting interferences

Over the course of a day, note down 'interferences' that you experience as you try and get on. You can use the examples provided below and/or you can add your own:

IT problems	Requests from peers
Supervisor	Daydreams
Coffee	Interruptions
Non-productive meetings	Going off at tangents
Red herrings	Noise
Being late	Being early
Forgetting things	Not making decisions
Procrastination	Text messages
Lacking motivation	Gremlins
Facebook	Emails
Too much to do	Friends

You can notice over the course of a week which ones tend to be most dominant and also see if other interferences emerge.

Just spotting interferences and naming them as such can go a long way towards deciding not to let them take hold during the PhD. However, sometimes that simply isn't enough and you need to give yourself permission to manage them.

Challenge: Permission to manage interferences

First, having identified your interferences, create a table (see below) and note those that appear to be down to you and those down to others. Which do you 'generate' and which appear to be interferences that happen because of other people?

Taking those that you 'generate', identify actions you could take to reduce them. For example, these might range from planning coffee time to only looking at Facebook in the evening, to playing music to block out other noise, to switching off your email.

Looking at those that appear to be down to other people, reflect first on what you might be able to take control of. What are you allowing to happen that enables other people to interrupt you? What actions could you take to stop that?

At one level examples might be: answering the phone, responding to texts, answering emails, leaving the door open.

At another level there may be some more difficult questions to reflect upon:

- What are you attributing more importance to when you allow other people's agendas to take over your own?
- When you allow other people to interrupt you, what impact is it having on you? And on others?
- Who are you being when you allow other people to interrupt you? How honest are you being with yourself and with them?
- What kind of boundaries do you set to protect your time, energy and space? Do others trespass too easily? What conversations might you need to have to re-establish the boundaries?

My interferences

My interferences	Down to me	Down to others	Action

Door closed, email off, phone on Silent, 'Do Not Disturb'

Christine was one of the more experienced PhD students in her department. Over time she had learnt the lab inside out, knew how to run the equipment and had a pretty good sense of how to keep things working. Her supervisor who oversaw the lab went away on a six-month sabbatical and asked Christine to stand in as a kind of lab manager while she was away. That all sounded good. During that period, new students came in, and other students started to have trouble with their experiments. At first it was fun. Christine enjoyed being useful, being the expert, and liked to be of service to her more junior peers. Gradually, however, the stress mounted as Christine realized she had become indispensable to them. Not only had they become dependent on her for sorting out the equipment, she was being contacted at all hours of the day for this, that and the other. It had got to the point where she couldn't find time to work on her own PhD, and when she did, she had lost focus.

The situation felt impossible. Christine reviewed her situation. She identified some obvious things she could do to stop the interruptions: not have email on, have the phone off and have 'Do Not Disturb' on her door. She let the lab group know that only in emergencies should they contact her. That worked to a point, except that definitions of 'emergencies' by her peers weren't quite what she meant!

Reflecting further, Christine realized that there was a deeper issue here. She got in touch with her supervisor via Skype and explained the problem. Her supervisor recognized how this had happened and identified a small budget to run some training for the whole group on how to work in the lab. Eventually, Christine was able to step back as all the people in the lab learnt how to use the equipment and help each other out. She re-found the focus she needed for her own work.

Busting procrastination (in all its guises)

> Never put off till tomorrow what you can do the day after tomorrow.
>
> (Attributed to Mark Twain, source unknown)

There are times, of course, when we love interferences! The interferences are just what we want: they help us put off doing that something – be it writing, analysis, phone calls, organizing fieldwork – that we know is going to take some energy or concentration or may even challenge us in ways we're not sure about. Of course, procrastination seems to be a common human condition, not just a symptom of PhD life. We find all sorts of reasons to, quite simply, put off doing what really needs doing. For whatever reasons, putting something off which needs doing in your PhD can somehow feel easier, in the short term, than actually doing it.

So, how to bust procrastination? Well, first, you absolutely need to go back to the start of this chapter before you go any further! If you want a quick fix to procrastination in your PhD, then you will find it; however, you need to have some good foundations in place first. You need to follow the review at the start of this chapter to make sure that, as a minimum, you have your self-doubting Gremlins in check, be clear on why you value the task at hand, have a sense of balance in mind, and be clear on what your goals are. You also need to have given yourself permission to focus, permission to put first things first, and permission to manage the interferences. And if you have done that, then you are ready to bust procrastination with some quick fixes.

Challenge: Strategies for busting procrastination

First, write down what you are putting off. This might be a long list of things you are avoiding (writing, analysis, contacting someone, completing something), or perhaps just one major task (a chapter, some reading, some fieldwork).

What is stopping you from making a start? Is this about a fear of some kind? A fear of failing or succeeding? Is it about your confidence to complete it? Is the enormity of the task too great to make a start feel worthwhile? Do you lack the creativity, the energy? Acknowledging what is stopping you is an important step.

For each thing you are putting off, answer the following questions:

- What are you gaining by waiting?
- How much energy are you expending in avoiding the task?
- What will happen in the long run if you keep putting this off?
- How will you feel once you've done it?
- What is at stake?

What small step needs to happen to make a start? What do you need to know or do? What space do you need to create? What will make starting more pleasurable (a drink next to you, music, something else)? What reward can you give yourself for making that start?

Build in some accountability. Is there someone you can tell you are going to do it, and who will hold you to account?

Note: you may have noticed patterns in your procrastination experience – a common trend, a common reason why you find yourself procrastinating. Pay attention to that. What would it mean to create some space to address the common issue?

Not sure how to start

Wei Long was a psychologist and felt he had a lifelong habit of procrastination. There were so many interesting things out there to learn about, jobs to do, people to catch up with. Indeed, it was amazing just how interesting they became when he was due to start new and (what felt like) different tasks. During his first year he realized he'd brought this habit well and truly with him. He'd put off writing a detailed research design until the last minute, had avoided starting to write a literature review until it had become scarily urgent, and was now stuck with how to present an end of year report (thank goodness the Olympics were on hand to distract him!). Wei Long noticed that, in fact, he didn't always procrastinate. It was the getting started that he struggled with. Indeed, he realized that he tended to put things off not because starting itself was difficult but because he didn't feel confident about what it was he was supposed to be doing. Standing back Wei Long realized that one strategy to try was to actually set some time aside to reflect on the task before trying to 'start'. By doing so, he could stand back and work out what he needed to know in order to feel confident to start. Putting energy into what he needed to know enabled him to have a clearer sense of the task at hand. The lifelong habit was gone . . .

Next steps to getting things done

This chapter has been about giving yourself permission to get things done for your PhD. What could be simpler? It's been about giving yourself permission to focus by creating a plan that means you can focus on the task at hand. It's been about giving yourself permission to get the important things done first. It's been about managing your interferences and taking control of what you can stop doing that is interrupting you. And it's been about busting procrastination. This all applies to every area of the PhD, whether it's about getting big jobs done, like writing chapters or reading heavy texts, or small yet significant tasks, like phoning a contact or letting your supervisor know something.

At various points in the chapter we've referred to other chapters that might be relevant in addressing some of the foundations of getting PhD work done: managing self-limiting beliefs, clarity about what is important to you, getting the right work–life balance that works for you, establishing the right goals, enabling a space to be creative, or even tapping into a sense of resilience. All the other chapters in this book can inform getting things done.

Finally, we want to invite you to reflect on the thought we raised at the start of this chapter about doing and being. What do you gain from being a person who gets things done? And how is this different to being the unfocused procrastinator?

Actions I have taken in this chapter	✔
Reviewed the foundations from Part I	
Made my 'permission to focus' Gantt chart	
Done the 'first things first' from my prioritized daily planner	
Reduced or eliminated at least one key interference from my day	
Started something important that I have been putting off	
Asked, 'What do I gain from being a person who gets things done?'	
Given myself a well-focused reward for doing everything on this checklist	

11

On your own? Building better relationships

> Embracing vulnerability and humility, let us declare our utter dependence on the Earth, and on each other: You are, therefore I am.
> (Satish Kumar, *You Are Therefore I Am: A Declaration of Dependence*, Totnes: Green Books, 2002: 205)

There is a classic narrative of the PhD experience as being an isolated, lonely process. As a PhD student you carry the burden of researching the depths of a topic that only you, your supervisor (potentially) and examiner (hopefully!) reads and understands – a topic about which very few people in the world are interested and yet which occupies your mind night and day. According to this narrative, you're on your own!

Relationships are, however, fundamental to the PhD process. You are in relationship with your supervisor(s), your peers, other people in your university, other academics and peers at other universities, with funders, sponsors, potential employers, your friends, family, and with other people in your life. Why stop there? You are in relationship with yourself and your emotions as well as with the PhD itself. The PhD experience is riddled with relationships. So let's start by declaring that your PhD experience is one of 'utter interdependence' on people and things around you.

Sometimes those relationships work well: supervisors engage with your work; peers stimulate you in debate and offer support; the department values your contribution; there is a vibrant research network that you are a part of; you have exciting relationships with stakeholders who are using your research; you have a flourishing social life; and you feel good about yourself and your relationship to your PhD. Sometimes, however, those relationships become a hindrance: relationships with supervisors can break down; your peers can be competitive or simply not interested in you; you can feel isolated and undervalued in the department; you don't have the confidence to talk about your study to the wider research community; your findings don't seem relevant to anything in the world; the stress of it all has led you to retreat from social life; you don't feel in touch with who you know you are; and your relationship with the PhD is one of angst.

This chapter is about how you relate to the people (and things) which are fundamentally crucial in helping to shape your PhD experience.

Questions to bear in mind while you read this chapter:

Who do your relationships enable you to be?

When is it crucial to be honest with yourself and others?

Who would you be able to become by engaging differently in your relationships?

We are inviting you to explore:

- your emotional wisdom: managing your relationship with your emotions and with other people's;
- the emergent relationship: identifying what your significant relationships need from you;
- challenging conversations: sharing expectations and learning to be real when it's tough.

You and your emotions

It's a rule of the world. When you know people are really at peace with who they are and what they do, they collaborate and want to help you to improve. . . .

(Javier Bardem, actor, interviewed in *The Guardian*, 13 October 2012: 42)

People often talk about the PhD roller-coaster of ups and downs. As we noted at the start of this book, doing a PhD is known to bring on the full range of emotions: excitement, boredom, being overwhelmed, fear, sadness, happiness, envy, guilt, terror, nervousness, anxiousness, depression, hatred, sorrow, delight, peace, and so forth. Some emotions seem to stick around that little bit longer, others seem to come and go. One moment all is well – you've had great feedback or a paper has been accepted – and the next it all falls apart as you find out someone else has published on your topic or your supervisor is leaving the university. We're sure you can add more examples here. Given that, it's surprising how rarely your emotions, or those of your supervisor, your peers, colleagues, etc. are explicitly acknowledged or explored as part of the PhD experience.

What we've offered through the book are various perspectives and challenges that suggest there is no need for a difficult emotional rite of passage as part of the PhD process. We think, however, that there is much to be gained from the PhD experience through more emotional awareness, particularly when it comes to relationships. So how are you today? You may remember in Chapter 1 we asked you to ask yourself how you are, and to keep doing so each day. We're asking you again now because emotions and how we manage them are so integral to relationships in the PhD experience and beyond.

We can build emotional wisdom. At other points in this book we've explored ways of 'managing' your emotions. In Chapter 7, for example, we offered ways to find the emotional state that you connect with feeling confident. If you need to approach a relationship with more confidence, you may need to build on some of the exercises from that chapter. However, there is also something specific about being in touch with your emotions in the context of relationships. Daniel Goleman, who has written extensively on managing emotions, points to how our 'emotional intelligence' (our capacity to be aware of, express and regulate our own emotions) is crucial for 'social intelligence' (that is, our capacity to be aware of and empathize with other people's emotions) (Goleman 1995). The combination of emotional and social intelligence, and learning how to use it, is what we call 'emotional wisdom'.

Emotional wisdom is about not only being aware of our emotions and those of other people, it is also about being able to make decisions based on that awareness. Employing your emotional wisdom means becoming more aware of the choices you are making about how you are being, and becoming more aware of how you are impacting on other people. In other words, as is the case throughout this book, this is an opportunity to take responsibility for your emotions in relation to your behaviour within relationships, i.e. an ability to notice, connect with, understand, express and take responsibility for your emotions.

The invitation contained in this chapter is for you to build better relationships within your PhD experience from a place of emotional wisdom. So that is where we start.

Challenge: Connecting with your emotions

It is only with the heart that one can see rightly; what is essential is invisible to the eye.

(Antoine de Saint-Exupéry, *The Little Prince*, London: Wordsworth Editions, 1995)

Here we want you to become more aware of your emotions specifically in the context of relationships with the people in your life.

First, think of a recent interaction with someone that left you frustrated, annoyed, hurt or generally wound up. Remember that interaction in as much detail as possible. Bring it alive:

- What were you talking about? What were you wearing? What could you see? What could you hear? What would somebody watching you have seen? What really mattered to you?
- Keeping your focus on that interaction: What were you feeling? What emotions were you experiencing? What sensations were you feeling in your body? What were those emotions saying about what you value?
- What emotions were you aware of, or assuming, in the other person?

The following words may help in describing emotions:

Bitter	Lonely	Dejected
Envious	Miserable	Cautious
Humble	Delighted	Hateful
Thrilled	Terrified	Brave
Frustrated	Horrible	Spiteful
Euphoric	Helpless	Shameful
Fearful	Captivated	Sorrowful
Desperate	Frustrated	Shocked
Hostile	Guilty	Other:
Angry		_____

Now, ask yourself: how were my emotions either helping or hindering me in this situation? How were those emotions affecting what I was doing, my body language, what I was saying, what I was perceiving? In what ways were my emotions positive and enabling, or negative and disabling?

Watch out for falling into the trap of automatically thinking emotions like anger or frustration are necessarily negative. Of course, they can be. Equally, though, when the 'energy' is understood, adjusted and channelled appropriately, such emotions can be enabling. And, of course, the converse is true for emotions typically considered positive.

Then, with an awareness of what your emotions enabled or hindered, re-enact the interaction in your mind. This time, do so from a perspective of how you would have preferred to have felt during that interaction. What different emotions would you like to have experienced? How would those emotions have impacted on what you did, said, heard, responded? What would you have done differently before, during and after the interaction? Ah, the wonders of hindsight!

Finally, think ahead to an interaction you are anticipating in the future. What do you want for this relationship, what's your goal? What can you learn from above about how you can approach that interaction with greater emotional wisdom? What do you need to do differently? Write down your answers – how will you make yourself accountable to what you need to do?

Note: we've hinted already that your PhD relationships are not just with other people. They are also with the things around you as well with your own emotions. Think about how angry people get at objects like computers that crash, at junk emails, at the car that won't start, at the puncture on the bike, and suchlike. And what about 'the PhD' itself, as something you have a relationship with? As you work through this chapter you can use the challenges creatively to think about such relationships and how your emotional wisdom can help.

Being with your friends

Brian's PhD had been a bit of a grind. Although he was passionate about computer science, the PhD process had felt like one long struggle. He'd had problems with his sponsoring organization when the main contact left. The software he had been using for his work was full of glitches. His supervisory team was also in conflict over the best direction for his work. Over time, Brian also realized that his relationships with his friends were also suffering. His conversations with his friends always seemed to be really heavy. Brian thought about this. He reflected on a recent interaction with a friend. He'd met the friend for a coffee on a day when things actually felt a little better. He'd had some success with the software and went feeling pretty good. As soon as he met his friend, however, he immediately started talking about how difficult the past few weeks had been. That set the tone for the conversation, a conversation about the doom and gloom of PhD life and supervision. Reflecting on how he'd been feeling, Brian remembered that although he was feeling good, he had brought to the conversation his default position of being negative. After all, feeling good could only be a temporary state! It suddenly struck Brian that most of his conversations with friends went this way. He decided that he needed to start his conversations differently, even if he was feeling bad. He set himself a goal for the next two conversations with friends to start with something good. In fact, he decided to phone a friend that evening and tell him all the good things about the day. Brian found that, having become more aware of the emotional energy he brought to conversations, once he shifted that energy, his friendships started to flourish for himself and his friends. He started to enjoy life, despite the inevitable problems that cropped up during his PhD.

What about the relationship's view on all this?

The emergent is unlike its components insofar as these are incommensurable, and it cannot be reduced to their sum or their difference.

(G.H. Lewes, *Problems of Life and Mind*, London: Trübner, 1875: 412)

When it comes to relationships in your PhD, it is all too easy to get caught in a 'blame game'. After all, when things aren't going right, there are lots of things to which or whom you can point the finger: your supervisors aren't giving you good feedback or don't appreciate what you are going through; the peers around you aren't interested in your topic; your collaborating industry partner won't release the data you need; your partner doesn't understand the pressure you're under; the university won't give you the office space you need; the computer keeps crashing; your inbox is too big to keep on top of, and so on. Sometimes you might be quite justified in your response to these people and things. The question is: how well does your response serve you, and how well does it serve the relationship?

Managing relationships is not all about the difficult ones, of course. You might be really excited to have found a new connection, someone who you feel you can really share some ideas. Yet how do you keep that spark alive, how do you make space for it in a busy schedule? Perhaps you want to rekindle or re-energize an old relationship that you really value but for which 'life' and the PhD have got in the way. What does that relationship need to keep it going? Or, maybe you find yourself in a tricky situation with a relationship that you have to engage with, and yet which feels really dysfunctional. What can you do to make it a more productive relationship? Whether this be with supervisors, peers, colleagues at other universities or friends, or even equipment, sometimes it can be hard to see just what you could do to make a difference.

So often when we think of relationships we think of ourselves and we think of the other people or things involved. Yet, what of the relationship itself, what if we also bring into account what it needs? What if we explore our role in relation to what the relationship needs? As an 'emergent' entity, i.e. something more than the sum of its parts, what might its perspective be? The next challenge does just that.

Challenge: An emergent relationship perspective

For this challenge you need to choose a relationship that you care about. That doesn't mean it is a relationship that you necessarily like. It means a relationship that, for whatever reason personal to you, it is important to improve. It needs to be a relationship that you are committed to doing something about.

To prepare, you need to be in a quiet space with three chairs in a triangle about 1.5 metres apart, some Post-it notes and paper. Jot the initial of the other person on a Post-it note and stick it on one of the chairs. Next, put your own initials on another Post-it note and stick this to one of the other chairs.

First, sit in your chair with your initials on and imagine the other person is sitting on the chair facing you. Imagine telling them what it is like for you being in this relationship. You might want to choose a recent interaction or talk more generally. Imagine telling them how you feel, what it is that bothers you, how things look from here, what it is you want from this relationship. Really capture what it's like for you to be in this relationship. Make notes if you wish.

Now, get up and step away from your chair and 'shake off' being you. Now sit on the chair with the other person's initials on it. Step into their shoes! See the world through their eyes, imagine being them. Be like them, how they sit, any mannerisms that embody who they are. Now think what they might want to say. What do they want to say about their experience? What do they want to express about how they are feeling? What is bothering them? How do things look for them in this relationship? What do they see you doing? How do they describe your behaviour? What pressures are they under? What do they want from the relationship? Again, make notes if you wish.

Note: it may take some practice to really see the world through the other person's eyes. If you slip back into the place of being you, then start this part again.

Now, stand up, jump around, take a few steps away.

Come back to the third chair and sit in this place. This is the relationship itself, emergent from the two people on the other two chairs. Imagine the relationship as a living entity, with feelings, opinions, needs. What is it like to be this relationship? Is it smooth, edgy, fragmented, exciting, frightening, vulnerable, strong? What does this relationship see you and the other person doing? How does it describe your behaviour? Now ask: what can this relationship see that the two people in the other chairs can't? What does it know that they don't know? What does the relationship want? What does it need from the two people to move in a more positive direction? Make notes if you wish.

Now, again get up and walk around. This time come back to your chair. Ask yourself: what is new here that I didn't see or know before? What do I need to do, what actions can I take to help move this relationship to a more positive place, to a better footing, to achieve better outcomes, perhaps even make it more nurturing? Be specific here. If you want to take responsibility for moving this forward, then set your goal for this relationship and commit to the steps you need to take to achieve it.

Note: as we mentioned earlier, the challenge above doesn't have to be restricted to relationships with people. Some PhD students have found it really helpful to do the same exercise with the PhD itself as the 'other'. The emergent then becomes the relationship between you and the PhD. It may seem odd to treat the PhD in this way. However, why not give it a go for a bit of fun? What is it like to be your PhD? What is it like to be the relationship between you and your PhD? What does each of you need?

Relating to your PhD

Javier was in the second year of his Chemistry PhD, and although in general it was going well and everything was on target, he felt awful. Though Javier did a lot of socializing and rock climbing which took him away from the world of the university, friends said he always looked like he had the weight of the world on his shoulders. He never seemed to relax fully into what he was doing. He always seemed a little on edge. After several coaching sessions, Javier was confident he wanted to be doing a PhD: he really valued what he was doing and he'd sorted out various Gremlins that were lurking around. Yet the heavy feeling didn't lift. In the next coaching session, he and the coach decided to focus on the PhD itself as a thing. Using the emergent relationship exercise, Javier sat with what it was like being him looking at his PhD. What emerged was a description of his PhD that was like a nagging child that always wanted attention and which he could never satisfy. When he sat with the PhD, what came to life was something different: a committed athlete who wanted his focus to be pushed further. When Javier stood in the emergent relationship perspective, something further emerged. What the relationship between him and his PhD wanted was a more defined, focused relationship between Javier and his PhD, one in which Javier's identify wasn't engulfed by the PhD. Sitting back in his own chair Javier felt an immediate sense of relief. His shoulders relaxed back and he sat up confidently. He said he realized now what he may have known already underneath, namely, that he needed to get more focused when he was with his PhD and to be clear on what he was trying to achieve in those moments. At the same time, rather like a firm parent, he needed to be firm and say 'no' to the PhD when it wasn't PhD time. By developing some more effective goal setting and also using visualizations to keep the PhD at more of a distance, Javier came back to life. His friends noticed almost instantly!

Changing conversations

Conversation about the weather is the last refuge of the unimaginative.

(Attributed to Oscar Wilde, source unknown)

At this point in the chapter we hope you've tapped into your emotional wisdom and taken a fresh look at one relationship or more from an emergent perspective. Through those challenges you may have identified changes you can make, and hopefully you've started to put those into practice. What we also imagine, however, is that there are some relationships where a conversation of a different kind might be needed. In particular, there may be some where it might be helpful to have shared expectations and others where you need to take a particularly brave approach.

If you look at guidance on being a supervisor, or even guidance on how to approach your supervisor, it often states that you need an upfront conversation about what your expectations of each other are. How often does that happen? How often have you had that conversation? If you have had the conversation, how well have you stuck to the agreement of expectations? Have you reviewed it recently? Who else do you have that kind of conversation with? As coaches, something we call 'contracting' is a crucial element of a coaching relationship. Contracting means agreeing how the coach and client are going to work together, what's OK and what isn't, and what the boundaries are of the conversation. Contracting is not a one-off event; it is an ongoing conversation, always up for renegotiation at the start of each session.

When you look at your PhD relationships, the question is: where do those relationships need some clearer agreements or a better understanding of each other and of your expectations of the relationship? All too often, misunderstanding, friction, or even conflict arise from the lack of clear expectations, wrong assumptions and having no agreed way of 'being' together. Of course, a few assumptions and some mind reading may work to a point. Yet so often the problem arises when there is too much misalignment. Perhaps you have agreed with your supervisor to respect each other's opinions, yet do you have a shared notion of what respect looks like and what sorts of behaviours that entails? Or maybe you have agreed with your partner that they support you during a tricky part of the PhD? Have you agreed what that will look like and what they need of you?

Challenge: A cooperative conversation

This next challenge is based on changing the conversation in a relationship where you think there is a need to gain some clarity of expectations. You need to choose a relationship where such a conversation feels safe for you to express your expectations. Where you sense conflict, you may need to refer to the next challenge and even consider a third party facilitator (see below).

First, you need to decide on the context to have this conversation: an informal chat while walking on the beach, over a glass of wine or beer, coffee shop, or in an office.

Start the conversation by voicing your expectations and your assumptions of the other person's expectations. You can start with the sentence, 'What I expect from you is . . .'. You can then say, 'What I think you expect of me is . . .'.

Now it's their turn to do the same (or they can start and you follow). The key thing is that you each share your expectations of each other, and also what you think the other person's expectations of you are.

You both need to do the following:

1 Share your thoughts in a balanced way, compare notes and be honest with each other. Don't rely on telepathy!
2 Take the time and the effort to clarify explicitly what each of you means by words like, for example, respect, love, cooperation, trust, support, supervision, etc.
3 Explore and clarify with each other the explicit behaviours needed to fulfil these expectations.

Next, use what you both discover from this conversation to form your new agreement for what you both need and how you will be together in this relationship.

The outcome will often be work in progress, so you don't need to look for a finished product. Actually, great value comes from keeping this as something to explore and update as part of the ongoing relationship.

Note: it is likely that a contract with a colleague would look and feel quite different to one with a partner or friend. The very nature of the type of conversation might also look very different. Similarly, how trusting (or otherwise) you are of the person you are engaging with may affect how explicit this conversation is. The key thing here is an underlying principle about sharing expectations. With a bit of creativity you can use this structure even if the other person is a little tricky to get on board, when they don't want to tango. For example, while walking to a meeting you might weave expectations into the conversation.

How is your supervisor?

Gloria was in the final year of her Anthropology PhD and was getting more and more frustrated with her supervisor's feedback. Gloria was drafting what she felt were near to final drafts of her data analysis chapters. However, whenever she got comments back from her supervisor, they always seemed to imply a need to rethink some funda-mental issues. She was starting to feel like she just wasn't capable. Something didn't make sense. Gloria had felt confident in her argu-ment, she felt she had been doing a thorough job of analysis and was feeling quite angry at the whole thing. In fact she started feeling quite angry at herself, too, for letting it get to her. Gloria had asked some friends to look over the comments and they, too, were a little surprised. Gloria had assumed that her supervisor knows best, so she was getting a little confused as to what was going on. She realized after some reflection that the situation was leading to confusion and anger, and she was losing her trust in her supervisor's ability. She had a good relationship with him, so decided to talk to him about how she was feeling. Her supervisor was immediately apologetic. They explored each other's expectations together. He reviewed the comments with her and said he'd got into a bad habit of making critical points whenever he could. He said he thought her work was excellent and that in the next drafts he would give her more positive feedback, focus on key areas where she needed to develop parts, and also keep in the background any 'questions' that she ought later to reflect upon (for example, in preparing for the viva). Actually, her supervisor was really grateful for the conversation because he realized this was happening with other students, too, and that he could make changes there as well.

Getting real

> While many fear 'real', it is the unreal conversation that should scare
> us to death.
>
> (Susan Scott, *Fierce Conversations: Achieving Success in*
> *Work and in Life, One Conversation at a Time.*
> London: Piatkus, 2002: 7)

Some of the conversations you are having or want to have within
your PhD experience are, quite simply, going to be awkward! The
previous challenge of a conversation about shared expectations will
feel quite easy with some people and almost impossible with others.
Awkward conversations come in all sorts of shapes and forms, and we
all have a different idea of what sort of conversation will count
as awkward. Through our coaching, we've found students wanting
conversations with a range of people (supervisors, other staff,
peers, friends, lovers, parents, etc.) that have been tricky. The topics
that become 'awkward' range from talking to supervisors about
their input, a change in research design, wanting a holiday; asking
parents for financial support or to listen more or to visit; talking
with friends about their demands on you during a stressful time; saying
'no' to people who are making too many requests of your time, and so
forth.

Challenge: Preparing for a difficult conversation

This challenge offers you a tool to work with in a difficult conversation.
It follows Susan Scott's book, *Fierce Conversations* (2002: 254). As
you prepare for this challenge, tap into your emotional wisdom and
spend time reflecting on what the emergent relationship needs from
you.

First, you need to prepare for the conversation. Set out a 60-second
opening statement to the conversation. This statement needs to
include: naming the issue clearly; a specific example that illustrates
the situation or the behaviour that you feel needs to change; how you
feel about the issue; what you think is at stake; what you see as your
contribution to the problem; an explicit indication that you want to
resolve it; and that you want to hear the other person's response.

Spend time listening to the other person's views. The emphasis here is really on listening to understand. You need to be confident not to have to be on the defensive. Your task here is to understand, and you can only do that if you suspend your own judgements while listening. Ask questions to clarify what they mean, paraphrase back to make sure you have understood. Let them know that you have understood their position, what they are saying and what is at stake for them.

Now, assess what is being learnt here. Have you left anything unsaid? Is there anything the other person has left unsaid? Does anything need more clarification?

Based on what you have learnt: where are you both now? What is required to move forward?

Next, make an agreement on the next steps you will each take and how you will hold each other accountable for taking them.

Note: in some conversations it may be that an agreement is difficult to reach and that the interim agreement is to seek third party mediation.

That's my work!

Zoe came into a coaching session feeling so cross. She'd just read a paper that her supervisor had presented to a recent workshop. In the paper, the supervisor had used her case study work to demonstrate his argument. The trouble was, while some reference to her PhD was made, this paper was presenting an argument that was very close to her own. If it was published, how could she then present her work using her own case study? Zoe wanted to go to the Dean and complain and ask them to do something. She wanted to change supervisors. She had lost all trust. Yet she was also confused. This supervisor had been fantastic up until this point. She had really valued his input. What could she do? Standing back, Zoe considered that her tendency in conflicts was to defer to someone else to sort it out while she would run away from directly being involved. This hadn't really served her well in the past and she realized this was a chance to do something different. Zoe engaged in a process of planning a potential conversation, and what she would say to start it off. She arranged to see her supervisor and, very assertively, said within 60 seconds what she had experienced, how it had impacted on her, what she felt was at stake, and her proposed solution. To her surprise, the supervisor was highly apologetic. He explained he hadn't intended to publish this piece and that it was a rushed paper he'd written on the train to the workshop. He hadn't realized it had gone online. He agreed with Zoe's proposal that they could produce a really good co-written paper that would draw on her case study, and that there were parts of her argument that she should save for her own paper. They found that they wrote really well together and Zoe took up a post-doc position with her supervisor.

Next steps to better relationships

The relationships you are in and taking responsibility for how you are with them are a crucial part of your evolving emotional wisdom. We started this chapter with your emotional wisdom in order to highlight the importance of being aware of emotions in relationships before taking particular actions or making certain decisions. In that sense, having also given you some tools for looking at relationships differently, for conversing about expectations and managing confrontations, that places you in an even better position to evaluate the wider PhD team and who needs to be a part of it. You may want to re-visit Chapter 6 and have another look at your perfect PhD team.

Clearly other chapters in the book also need to play a part here – after all, they all contribute to your emotional wisdom. For your relationships to be what you want them to be, you need to have a clear sense of what you value and to be aware of any interrupting Gremlins that throw doubt on what is possible. It may be that your relationships need you to reflect on the balance in your PhD experience. They may need you to have clearer goals and a steadier focus. Perhaps they need you to be working from a place of self-confidence. Indeed, you may need to apply some creative thinking to your relationships. The important thing is to recognize that, in all these areas, relationships are a key part of the jigsaw, and that 'how you are' is a key part of the emergent relationships you are involved in.

Actions I have taken in this chapter	✓
Explored my emotional wisdom and its impact on my relationships	
Established clearer expectations within a relationship	
Taken steps to confront a difficult conversation	
Taken action to benefit a relationship as a result of the emergent relationship perspective	
Identified which chapters of the book might also be helpful	
Given myself an emotionally wise reward for doing everything on this checklist	

12

Too many knockbacks and brick walls?
Building your PhD resilience

> You may have a fresh start at any moment you choose, for this thing
> that we call 'failure' is not the falling down, but the staying down.
> (Mary Pickford, actress and co-founder of
> United Artists, source unknown)

Sometimes during a PhD there seem to be too many knockbacks or too many brick walls – it all just feels very wrong. Crisis looms. Life feels out of place. People's responses tend to vary. Some grin and bear it, put on a brave face, ride the storm: somehow or another, whether through endurance, stoicism or sheer good luck, the PhD will get finished. Others find distractions through different forms of escape or time out, enabling them to come back with a fresh look or a new outlook, or feeling worthy having organized an event for your research group! Some PhD students deny there is a problem, keeping on doing what they are doing, pushing themselves to do more of it. Sometimes that works. Sometimes they get caught out by the storm, finding themselves in a bigger crisis than they realized. At its worst, whatever response they adopt, PhD students often describe a background of anxiety, vulnerability, fatigue, being overwhelmed, failure, despair, frustration, or even ill-health. When prolonged, this may lead for some to a generalized anxiety, perhaps even to depression, burnout or physical illness. All in all, the PhD can at times feel like a very serious, weighty, business indeed!

Resilience might just be the antidote! Strategies for building PhD resilience vary because resilience manifests in different ways, from one situation to another and from one person to another. Resilience for you might be having the staying power to bounce back and keep going, despite the knockbacks and challenges that the PhD and life in general throw at you. Your PhD resilience might be about adaptability to different situations, being willing to go with the flow even if it's not quite what you expected. Finally, being resilient throughout your PhD might be about a personal process of learning, growing and transformation through adversity. Resilience can be all these things.

Whether or not you are in a specific moment of crisis, are experiencing prolonged stress, or are feeling reasonably strong, this chapter invites you to explore your resilience. At the heart of this is living true to your values and being able to create choices. Even when things look really bad, they look quite different when you identify choices and evaluate those choices from a place of being true to yourself, of knowing what really matters to you. In this sense, all the chapters of the book provide foundations for building your resilience. At the same time, there are specific strategies for dealing with crisis that we offer in this chapter, strategies which may or may not be relevant to you right now and yet may prove vital. What we encourage and indeed challenge you to do, is to read this chapter with, following Mary Pickford, a fresh start, a fresh look, and to see where it takes you.

How can you stay true to yourself through everyday ups and downs?
Who are you being when your resilience is strong?

In this chapter we will explore:

- taking responsibility for the roots of your responsibility, now;
- choosing to see things in a different way, however bad they first appear;
- getting more done by doing less, letting go and standing back;
- recharging your energy.

A brief caveat: this chapter is written from a coaching perspective on building resilience. Should you have concerns about your mental health, we recommend you seek professional advice.

Roots to resilience

> Imagine a tree receiving nourishment from the earth, the water, and the minerals. With all that it takes in, it nourishes the branches and leaves and creates flowers . . . if we disturb the tree's roots, so that they are not in touch with the soil, the tree can't get the nutriments it needs to make flowers and fruits.
>
> (Thich Nhat Hanh, *Peace Begins Here: Palestinians and Israelis Listening to Each Other*, Berkeley, CA: Parralex Press, 2004: 39)

In building resilience for your PhD, there is a need to establish some strong roots at the same time as stretching out to reach for new challenges, to learn and grow. Part I of this book ('Saying "yes" to the perfect PhD day') shows how to build a foundation, a root structure, for being resilient. Saying 'yes' is not about everything happening as you want it to, or things going exactly to plan, never going wrong. Saying 'yes' is about knowing that, however adverse the situation, you are approaching it in a way that honours your values. Part I provides a tool kit, a navigation aid, to approach each day in a way that works for you, a way that holds you to account and makes you fully responsible for bringing your values to life each day.

Your resilience will sometimes grow as a response to the different challenges you face. Indeed, crisis situations might be a wonderful opportunity to really test out your tool kit and make it even better! In addition, specific situations may require additional tools. Building your resilience may well require some further attention to the balance in your life (Chapter 6), to the habits through which you are maintaining confidence (Chapter 7), to your sense of achievement through goal setting (Chapter 8), to whether you are getting things done (Chapter 10), to whether you feel blocked by a lack of creativity (Chapter 9) and to the relationships you have in place (Chapter 11).

Throughout all these chapters we have challenged you to make changes in ways that serve you well. Studies have repeatedly shown that stress is related to feeling a loss of control within daily life, a loss of taking responsibility. This can be true in the PhD process too. It is easy to blame supervisors, equipment, peers, 'the system' or any other target other than yourself (perhaps even the authors of this book!). And it's easy to spend a lot of energy worrying about things. And yet, as we noted in the book's Introduction, many people, even in the face of the most extreme circumstances, have managed to take responsibility for their own experience, despite what is happening to them. Victor Frankl, as we cited in the Introduction, says this is the last of the human freedoms, the ultimate freedom that cannot be taken away.

Before we go further then, there is a need to check in with what you might be able to take responsibility for now.

Challenge: A small step to taking control of worry

Grant me the serenity to accept the things I cannot change,
the courage to change the things I can,
and the wisdom to know the difference.
(Prayer attributed to twentieth-century American
theologian, Reinhold Niebuhr, source unknown)

Make a list of everything that concerns you about your PhD, the things you worry about or fuss over. Note these concerns as headings. Here are some examples of things you might note down, but please choose your own: feeling tired; lack of money; writing blocks; stressed supervisor; university policies; feeling isolated; not enough time; understanding the literature; experiment not working; poor IT support; not knowing enough; future career . . .

Now draw a big circle with a smaller circle inside. Now, taking each concern or aspect from your list, answer the following question: do I have control or some influence over this? This is not a moment for in-depth analysis: your quick hunch answer will do perfectly! If the answer is 'yes', write the concern in the inner circle. If the answer is 'no', write it within the space between the inner circle and the outer circle.

Look at everything you have placed in the space between the inner circle and outer circle. Certainly all these aspects concern you but if you cannot control or influence them in some way, does worrying about them really help? For now, acknowledge them as concerns and accept them (acceptance is not the same as agreement). On the other hand, you may just have realized there is something (however small) you can do, in which case shift it to the inner circle.

Now look in the inner circle and pick one aspect that you are most drawn to. How can you influence or control this in some way? What can you take responsibility for? What action, however small, can you do that could make a difference? Plan a course of action.

And, finally, don't stop there: you can continue to use this principle whenever you feel you need to.

It's the world's fault!!!

Charlotte was doing a PhD in linguistics. Now in her third year, she was very fed up with a continued sense of struggle. Everything, it seemed, was against her. Things always seemed to go wrong: her computer would crash, library books were recalled when she hadn't finished with them, her supervisor was stressed with a heavy teaching term just when she needed more input, and she was worried that she wasn't paying attention to her diet. Over time Charlotte seemed to have got into a habit of blaming everything around her and spending a lot of energy worrying about what might go wrong next. Charlotte reached her limit when she had been awake all night worried about what she'd do if her supervisor went off ill. She explained it all to a friend, who said, 'What's the point of worrying about something you can't do anything about?' Charlotte listed all the things that were bothering her and then completed the exercise above. She saw that, over a period of time, she'd taken to focusing her energy on worrying about things that she could do nothing about, while also feeling anxious about things she'd been ignoring and *could* do something about. As she put some plans into action and took control of the things she could, Charlotte found something shifted. She found that not only did 'getting on with things' feel better, but it also meant she spent less time worrying about the things she could do nothing about.

Are things really that bad?

> Instead of seeing the rug as being pulled from under us, we can learn to dance on a shifting carpet.
> (Thomas F. Crum, quoted by Susan Jeffers, *End the Struggle and Dance with Life: How to Build Yourself up When the World Gets You Down*. New York: St Martin's Press, 1996: 184)

PhD life certainly has the potential to feel like the rug has been pulled from under you. Indeed, it can feel like the rug might be pulled away from you at any moment if you don't keep your eye on the ball! You write such a well-crafted argument, and your supervisor puts red pen all over it. Your best-laid plans for fieldwork fall apart when the equipment doesn't arrive. Your analysis won't come together because of a glitch in the software. Just when you thought you had a unique contribution, out comes a new book on your topic. You thought you'd mastered a particular theory, only to meet someone who knows it better and you feel like you've only just begun. We're sure you can add to this list!

There is another story we can tell for each of the examples listed above. It is a story about excitement and vitality. What an honour to be pushed further than you thought was possible with your writing! What a gift to learn the skills and aptitude to adapt your plans to changing circumstances, perhaps in ways that will make the work better! What fun to be the first person to have pushed the software to its limit, to have engaged with the programmers about how to improve it! The excitement and privilege of being at the forefront of your topic, part of a community pushing the boundaries of knowledge as you write, enabling you to take the ideas even further and to really contribute to a 'live' debate. To be able to converse with people so engaged in your area of interest, able to teach you more than you could possibly get from the books alone.

You can't change what has happened in your PhD or necessarily some of what is going to happen. What you *can* change is your response. You are obliged to do certain things in the future – such as ultimately submit the thesis and defend it in the viva! You are *not* obliged to feel about those things in any particular way.

Challenge: Changing the story

Reframing, that is, changing the meaning or perspective of an experience or event you have faced or that you are facing, in ways that serve you well, is a bit of an art that takes practice. In the words accredited to the inventor Thomas A. Edison, 'I have not failed. I've just found 10,000 ways that won't work.' Try the following to notice the difference.

First, *pick an event* that has happened that didn't go as well as you would have liked. Maybe some feedback you received, a presentation you gave, some writing, lab work, or fieldwork.

Then, pick *the current frame:* What meaning are you making of this? What are you making this event say about you and about what is possible? What are you saying the event implies about your PhD? What assumptions about causation are you making? How much are you over-generalizing what this event means to encompass how it could affect other things in the future?

Now, *the reframe:* What alternative perspectives or meanings exist? Try answering some of the following:

- What else could this mean?
- Who are you assuming is seeing the event in this way?
- What is there in this event or experience that could be useful?
- What is there for you to learn from this?
- What did you do well?

The next stage is *taking control of your thoughts and choosing what will serve you best*. None of these meanings are true in and of themselves. They are different perspectives (no matter what the Gremlins might try to tell you). Which perspective will serve you best? What do you want to choose this event to mean?

Finally, *taking responsibility:* What will choosing this meaning enable you to you take responsibility for, and what will you do next?

'POTS'

Will (this really was Will!) hit a moment of crisis in his PhD when, every time he tried to write, he'd realize there was more and more he didn't understand about the social theory he was working with. He'd reached a point where his confidence was so low he really started to doubt whether he'd be able to finish the PhD. Will talked this through with Jeff (this really was Jeff!). What emerged in the conversation was that Will wanted to feel confident in his material, and to be sure he covered all the bases, which was why he kept seeing more and more to be covered. What mattered to him was being clear about what he knew and, if there were areas he wasn't sure of, at least know why he didn't need to pursue them, rather than them feeling like a big unknown. The trouble Will was having was how to plan the final stages of his PhD to ensure he finished on time. Following a conversation with Jeff, the problems were reframed from 'STOP' into 'POTS': productive opportunities for thoroughness. This surprisingly simple reframing shifted 'POTS' from being something that felt heavy and unsolvable to manageable problems that felt much lighter and with which Will could confidently engage.

Notice that reframing is not an issue of optimism or pessimism, as some PhD students have queried in workshops. Both optimism and pessimism imply a perspective about the future in response to the perceived meaning of events and what it is assumed will follow. These are ways of thinking and you can choose your thoughts. So discover how it feels to reframe a problem; notice what it enables in you. See how you feel when you make a choice about how you (re)frame events – past, present and future.

Examples of reframing in your PhD

'My fieldwork hasn't produced what we thought it would. This always happens to me . . . .' could be reframed as: *My fieldwork has produced some surprising results. It's an exciting opportunity to think about my contribution.*

'My supervisor keeps giving my writing really negative comments. They don't see me as an equal . . .' could be reframed as: *I get such thorough critique from my supervisors, I'm confident I've covered all the angles.*

'In the presentation they asked me such difficult questions. I can't ever respond quickly enough . . .' could be reframed as: *People really engaged with my research at a deep level. They must have been interested in it, and now I've got some great ideas to follow up.*

'I'm struggling to understand the reading. I don't know my subject well enough . . . .' could be reframed as: *There is so much I'd like to learn; this is a chance to prioritize what the essentials are.*

'I just can't see how to get it all done, I always take on too much . . .' could be reframed as: *There is so much I want to do and am capable of, so I need to really decide what is important to me.*

'I always take longer than everyone else to do it . . . .' could be reframed as: *I'm a perfectionist and like to make sure I've done a good job.*

Letting go

[T]o start doing things a new way, you have to end the way you are doing them now; and to develop a new attitude or outlook, you have to let go of the old one you have now. Even though it sounds backwards, endings always come first. The first task is to let go.

(William Bridges, *Transitions: Making Sense of Life's Changes*. Reading, MA: Addison-Wesley, 1980: 80)

How do you respond when things are not going well in your PhD? Do you get busy hoping somehow that by doing 'more' things will move forward? However exhausted you might feel, this strategy assumes that as long as you put in the hours, this PhD thing will happen. Do you get busy doing other things, perhaps giving your tutees extra input, organizing events in the department or a social gathering? This strategy sometimes helps people to feel worthy, yet the background anxiety remains as the PhD doesn't move forward. Or perhaps you develop a stress-induced depression, and retreat from the PhD and other activities? With this strategy, perhaps you feel lost, not really knowing what to do, constantly thinking over all the possibilities, playing mental ping-pong, feeling guilty and full of self-doubt.

What if you were to try a different strategy, to take an active step back from the urgency of the work, a letting go, in order to then move forward? PhD students find this very hard to do. Gremlins might be saying, 'You mustn't step back in case you forget something' or 'There's no time for reflection: do, do, do!', or 'If I'm not seen to be busy, people will think I'm not working hard', and so on. And yet, when PhD students do it, when you do step back from the immediacy of the ever-so-important, overbearing PhD, so many more possibilities can become available. In coaching sessions, PhD students often describe how, when they find that distance by stepping back, they start to see the wood for the trees, they can see where they need to focus their energy, they feel their creative juices start flowing again, they feel rejuvenated, and they find they get 'the PhD' in perspective with the rest of life. All by stepping back and doing less!

Challenge: A step at stepping back

An old woman, when asked why she was always cheerful, replied: 'Well, I wear this world just as a loose garment.'
(Unknown, quoted by Susan Jeffers, *End the Struggle and Dance with Life: How to Build Yourself up When the World Gets You Down*. New York: St. Martin's Press, 1996: 20)

This exercise lets you explore what stepping back and getting some distance from your PhD might enable for you.

Think about your PhD. What do you see? Get a vivid image. Perhaps you see a lab, books, words on a page, your desk – or something different.

Hold the image you have in your mind's eye and notice how this makes you feel both emotionally and in your body. Perhaps you are experiencing sweaty palms; excitement, fear, a beating heart, a hot flush, overwhelming feelings, sick, heavy shoulders, freaked out, relaxed, hot under the collar, cold feet, etc.

Keep the image of your PhD vivid. Now pretend you have a 'picture editor' and try out some editing! With each edit, notice how your feelings and emotions change.

- Make the image black and white.
- Make it more colourful.
- Make it expand.
- Make it shrink.
- Make it appear closer.
- Move it appear further away.
- Make it blurred and fuzzy.
- Make it sharp and clear.
- Move the image to a different place, left, right, up, down, behind you, etc.
- Add some movement, keep it still.
- Add sound, e.g. your favourite song or piece of music.
- Speed it up, slow it down.
- Add a cartoon character.
- Change anything you like!

Be playful and experiment in how you change the image.

Now edit the image until you experience peace of mind. Sit with that image in a place that allows you to feel comfortable with your thoughts and feelings. Keep your breathing calm – count in for eight, breathe out for eight.

Holding this new image of your PhD what do you notice? What is important here? What do you need to let go of?

Stepping back and letting go is an invitation to taste getting a little distance from your PhD, and to see what this might enable for you. This might sound counter-intuitive: how can we be suggesting you step back and engage in letting go when so much is at stake? How will the PhD move forward if I stand back from it? How will my writing get done if I let go? How will all the jobs that need doing get done if I detach myself from it? Notice how your Gremlins might be raising the stakes and, if you need to, let go of some Gremlins as well.

Letting go of the problem which then becomes the solution

Kadia was an anthropology student, half way through her second year. She'd been following a 'text book' model of research in which she had done a thorough literature review and designed a perfect project plan. When she went out into the field to work with an indigenous group, she found that things weren't really matching up. The literature turned out to be a little outdated in terms of how this group had adapted to a changing political and environmental context. She also found out that her research plan wasn't going to work – the informants she'd hope to meet were not forthcoming and there seemed to be resistance to engaging with her. At first, Kadia was so fed up, she felt the whole thing was a disaster. She'd come back to her university and was feeling quite depressed. She read more and more and yet wasn't finding a way through. Her friends encouraged her to take some time out and get some distance from her work. In a 'eureka moment' while having a go at rock climbing, it struck Kadia that the problem was the solution. Although she couldn't see it at the time, she considered that the problem with the literature presented the perfect opportunity for her PhD: her contribution could be a new account of the changed practices and impacts of political and environmental change. She also realized that the problems she had with informants was related to this change and she could use that as part of her conversation with them. Kadia saw her initial reading meant she now knew where the gaps were and her research plan had provided a good basis from which to have been surprised by the field. Nothing was lost, all was well, and Kadia re-entered the field and found the informants opened up.

The paradox here is that by stepping back and letting go you can become more present and getting the things that matter done becomes so much easier. As Jon Kabat-Zinn writes, 'Non-doing simply means letting things be and allowing them to unfold in their own way. Enormous effort can be involved, but it is graceful, knowledgeable, effortless effort, a "doerless doing", cultivated over a lifetime' (2004: 44). As the saying goes, there are two ways to hold a coin: grasp it tight in your hand, or let it sit on the flat of your palm.

Controlled folly

David had got to a point where his PhD in water management was really weighing him down. He knew that letting go was important, that he was taking his work far too seriously. He felt like the weight of the world was on his shoulders. A friend said to him that perhaps he needed to apply some 'controlled folly' and to read a rather odd book by an anthropologist, Carlos Castaneda. David was totally confused and did some reading. The term 'controlled folly' emerges when Castaneda is undergoing training in shamanism! The puzzle Castaneda was trying to make sense of was this: how and why did a sorcerer, who could 'see' realities beyond the limited assumptions of our everyday world, still manage to engage in life in a practical way, when apparently that practical world is of irrelevance? Castaneda reports the following response when he asks his teacher Don Juan Matus, a 'man of knowledge', just what controlled folly is:

'Please tell me, Don Juan, what exactly is controlled folly?'
   Don Juan laughed loudly and made a smacking sound by slapping his thigh with the hollow of his hand.
   'This is controlled folly!' he said, and laughed and slapped his thigh again.
   'What do you mean . . .?'
   'I am happy that you finally asked me about my controlled folly after so many years, and yet it wouldn't have mattered to me in the least if you had never asked. Yet I have chosen to feel happy, as if I cared, that you asked, as if it would matter that I care. *That* is controlled folly!'

(Carlos Castaneda, 1990: 84)

In other words, for David, controlled folly was about acting as if something really matters, yet also paradoxically, at the same time, being able to stand back and treat it as something of an illusion. Here the prompt of 'controlled folly' was just enough for him to be able to let go of some of the weight and yet focus intently on what he was doing. Over time this allowed space for David to explore more aspects of 'letting go' and to start to really enjoy himself again.

Recharging

'I have so much to accomplish today that I must meditate for two hours instead of one.'

(Attributed to Ghandi, source unknown)

Keeping your energy up isn't always easy in a PhD, especially when the PhD carries over into the rest of life. Of course a PhD is challenging and can test you to your limits at times. It might be disappointing if it didn't! Must it, though, undermine your general sense of self and well-being? How often does 'THE PHD' dominate how you are mentally, emotionally and physically? Does the PhD undermine your very essence? (Note, we think of 'essence' as your 'sense of self'. For some people this might be their sense of vision and purpose, for others this may be about 'who they are' and their values, for others this might be about their sense of spirit.)

It can be useful to take stock of where your energy is going. There's not much point putting the heating on if you haven't closed the door! When you are feeling drained during your PhD, where is your energy going, where is your vitality draining away? For some PhD students it can be a case of feeling physically drained after spending long days in the field and working late into the night writing up the notes. It might be that such long hours leave you mentally drained as you work to finish the analysis while it's all fresh in your head. Or you might feel mentally drained from all the anxiety and worry about what might go wrong.

Challenge: Plugging the leaks

What would it be like if you could conserve more energy for the most important things? The challenge is to find how you might be letting your power leak and your energy escape, what day-to-day stressors are draining you of zest, and then to see where you could take control and plug some leaks.

First, create a checklist for yourself of habits that may leak energy. How often do you spend time indulging in any of the list below? Tick them off through the day or over a few days. Of course, add any others that come to mind.

Trying to be better than   Wishing things could be different
Feeling not as good as   Telling untruths to yourself/others

Being pessimistic	Thinking about how unfair things are
Judging yourself	Thinking about revenge
Pleasing friends	Thinking of lost opportunities
Regretting old failures	Thinking of resentments
Pleasing people at work	Trying to control others
Pleasing your family	Worrying about what might happen
Replaying conversations in your head	Looking good
Replaying old hurts	Blaming others

(Adapted from Carol Adrienne, *The Purpose of Your Life: Finding Your Place in the World Using Synchronicity, Intuition, and Uncommon Sense.* New York: Eagle Brook, 1998: 95)

Which are the most significant leaks for you? Perhaps observing them has been enough for something to shift?

Note: to complete this challenge and the next you need a number of pieces of card (postcard size), some red and some green.

Identify the leaks you want to plug and write each one on a separate red card. Keep these safe.

The next challenge is about what you do to recharge your vitality, to boost your energy during your PhD. Mentally, physically, socially as well as in your essence, what space do you give to recharging the batteries? In his book, *The 7 Habits of Highly Effective People* (1989), Stephen Covey tells of a woodcutter who has so much wood to cut that he doesn't have time to stop and sharpen his saw. Instead he carries on, head down, exhausted and cutting more and more slowly as the saw becomes blunter and blunter. What is the equivalent in relation to your PhD? When do you plough on, only to work more and more slowly, when a recharge would be more helpful?

Challenge: Steps to recharging

First, ask 'How well am I looking after my physical self?' Do you get enough food, water, exercise, sleep and rest? Think of your daily habits and behaviours which nurture your physical self: what are the things that recharge you? Write your answers on the green cards (one per card). Are there ways in which you undermine your physical health, habits or behaviours that may harm you? Write your answers on the red cards and add these to the red cards from plugging leaks.

Now, repeat the above, for your mental and emotional power and energy. Finally, repeat for your sense of essence.

Note that the red cards from plugging leaks may impact on all levels: physical, mental and essence.

Now put your red cards together into a pile (the leaks and things that undermine your energy and vitality) and your green cards into a pile (things you are doing that are positive for your energy and recharge your vitality).

Look at all the 'green' things you are currently doing and select *four* that you want to do more of or build on in some way.

Consider all the 'red' things and select *four* that you would like to stop doing or do less of. Aim for a balance from across all the four areas – physical, mental, emotional and essence.

You now have eight cards. Take each one and write a three-step plan on the back of the card describing how you will accomplish progress in that area. Be creative, try something new or different. On the front, write the first step that you will commit to taking this week.

Finally, how will you hold yourself accountable? Who could you share this with who will support you in this endeavour?

The PhD power nap!

Many a famous person in history has attested to the efficacy of a power nap as a way to recharge and, indeed, to manage stress. All it takes is 10 to 15 minutes and, with practice, can be a great way to refresh. You can find many techniques for how to take a power nap and this is one. Lie or sit in a comfortable place. Set an alarm for 10 minutes. Take a deep breath, and as you breathe out, say, 'My body is at peace' and let a sinking feeling come over your body. Take a second deep breath and say, 'My mind is at peace' and let a light feeling come over your mind. Then take a third breath, and say, 'I am fully at rest.' Then sink into it until the alarm goes off.

Next steps to building your resilience

This chapter brings together the underlying message of the whole book: the roots to your personal PhD resilience are to be found in how you choose to live each day, true to your values and your purpose, and how accountable you are to yourself for that. Such roots may themselves adapt and grow. Whether such growth happens, and how, will depend on how you respond to the events and circumstances you experience. This chapter has offered some additional ways to deal with those events that may at first appear as knockbacks or brick walls.

Some of what you find in this book and in this chapter may offer a very different way of approaching things. New ways can take time to develop. One of our coachees offered a useful metaphor for this:

> It's like you have a wood and in that wood there is a well-trodden path that is easy to follow to get to the other side. However, you know that, in the long run, that well-trodden path isn't the most helpful to get to the other side because it takes you further away from where you really want to be. You start to create a new path. This is hard work at first – you have to flatten down all the undergrowth, move rocks aside, etc. At first, this new path isn't so easy to walk on and you get constantly tempted down the old one. Over time, however, with some persistence, the new path starts to smooth out. Eventually, growth on the other path means that the new path becomes the smoother route, the more normal route, the easier route. And it takes you where you want to go.

So the invitation in this chapter is to keep working on finding the path that works for you: How wedded are you to the ways you currently do things? Do you want to find an alternative to the path you are on?

Other chapters in the book will be important. In Part I, Chapter 5 we offer a way to approach each day that will set you up for a smoother pathway. The subsequent chapters then encourage you to explore different ways of being that may serve to energize you in different ways, to give you the resources to be creative, confident, motivated, focused, in relationship, and with the right balance.

Actions I have taken in this chapter	✔
Used the circles of influence and concern to put things in a better perspective	
Reframed the meaning of an experience in a more useful way	
Made distance from my PhD when I need to by letting go and standing back	
Plugged at least one gap to stop leaking energy	
Made time to recharge mentally, physically, socially and in my essence	
Reviewed the chapters in the book to help build my resilience	
Given myself a recharging reward for doing everything on this checklist	

Part III

Leadership in your PhD and beyond

13

The leader in you?
Finding the authenticity to write your own story

This is the true joy in life, the being used for a purpose recognized by yourself as a mighty one; the being thoroughly worn out before you are thrown on the scrap heap; the being a force of Nature instead of a feverish selfish little clod of ailments and grievances complaining that the world will not devote itself to making you happy.

(George Bernard Shaw, 'Epistle Dedicatory to Arthur Bingham Walkley', in his 1903 play, *Man and Superman: A Comedy and a Philosophy*)

The core message of this book is that, however hard and challenging the issues that your PhD and its process throw up, there are always choices you can make. Those choices might be about the things you do, about the perspectives you take, or about the way you want to be within a situation. The questions we have posed invite you to reflect on the extent to which the choices you are making uphold what really matters to you. We have explored this in relation to your bigger picture, your core values and how those translate into the right balance in your PhD experience. To take this further and to really think in depth about what this means, we offer this chapter to explore another underlying question: when you change what you do, take a fresh perspective or approach a situation in a different way, how authentic are you being?

To explore being authentic we think it's important to reflect on leadership and your 'inner leader'. Leadership comes in all sorts of shapes and forms. It is a concept with all sorts of connotations. There are hundreds of textbooks on the subject and thousands of models. Indeed, the word 'leadership' may awaken your Gremlins who will be holding warning flags about arrogance, power, success, failure, control, etc. However, we want to suggest it's worth reflecting on the idea that you are 'leader' of your PhD experience. True, you may have more or less directive supervisors and you may not feel you have a team to direct. Nonetheless though, not only is it you that must produce the text that will be the PhD, the message of this book has been that it is also you that can take charge of how you want the PhD experience to be. To add to the previous question then: how authentic is the leader in you?

While leadership and authenticity are big topics, this final chapter is brief because the foundations of your authentic leadership are embedded throughout the book. Where Part I identifies core foundations from which to build the perfect PhD day within which you connect to your bigger picture and wider values, Part II brought these to life in particular themes, namely, balance, motivation, focus, creativity, relationships, and resilience. Each of those themes brought out different resources or capabilities within you. The authentic leader in you then is that person who can harness the resources you need to address the challenge at hand in a way that feels true to yourself, that honours who you are and how you want to be in the world.

> Who is your inner leader?
>
> What undermines your authenticity?
>
> What will being more authentic say about you as a person?

As a way of reviewing what you have done and looking forward to how you might approach what comes next beyond the PhD experience, this chapter invites you to do the following:

- explore how the authentic leader in you shines through each day;
- identify the inner allies that support your authentic leadership;
- write your own PhD experience story.

How does your authentic leader shine through each day?

That inner voice has both gentleness and clarity. So to get to authenticity, you really keep going down to the bone, to the honesty, and the inevitability of something.

('Authentic Voice: an interview with Meredith Monk', *Mountain Record: The Zen Practitioner's Journal.* Dharma Communications, Summer, 2004: 54–8)

If you've followed through on the challenges we've offered, you will be doing things differently than when you first opened up this book. You will also at various times have needed to work with quieting down your Gremlin voice. If that is the case, it's because you have made some choices to make those changes. And, which is the crucial bit, those choices will be informed by what you hold to be important, what you value in your PhD experience and beyond. In other words, the changes you have made enable you to become more authentic in your everyday experience. One way to think about authenticity is as the alternative inner voice to that of the Gremlin. The authentic inner voice is the one that works from what you value, what you hold to be true to yourself, to your bigger picture. In following this book, we hope that you have come closer to your voice of your authenticity.

We don't intend a philosophical diversion into the problems of defining the meaning of authenticity. For us, the point is that the language of authenticity points to a sense of awareness about your honesty and integrity in relation to how you are being and what you are doing. The chapters of this book all point to different contexts in which during your PhD experience and beyond you may feel more or less authentic. In some contexts you may feel you are more of a 'fake' and in others you may feel the 'real deal'. We are not claiming that being authentic is easy all the time. Sometimes it can be hard, especially when it impacts on people around you.

> **Challenge: What will the authentic leader in you be doing consistently?**
>
> Identify six to ten behaviours that you will be doing consistently each and every day through your PhD experience and beyond that mean you

are living authentically. These stem naturally from what you have learnt about yourself through the process of engaging with this book.

Write these down, treasure them, keep them safe. They are your guide to the future.

Looking at your list: which require more attention? Where today do you want to become more authentic? Identify an action, or way of being, that will help you achieve that.

Note, by now you know what works for you. Would identifying a score and goal for authenticity work for you? Do you need a daily reminder of some kind? How can you treasure these behaviours and bring them to life each day? Some form of accountability? Something else?

Though fulfilling, being authentic isn't always easy. Sometimes it needs to be learnt. And sometimes it can mean hard work, making difficult decisions, having challenging conversations or letting go of things that might at the time feel painful. What resources then might you need to be authentic, what form of leadership might that require?

Your inner allies

My ally is the little smoke, but that doesn't mean that my ally is in the smoking mixture, or in the mushrooms, or in the pipe. They all have to be put together to be to the ally, and that ally I call little smoke for my reasons.

(Carlos Castenada, *A Separate Reality*, New York:
Simon & Schuster, 1990: 44)

One way of understanding this book is that it has been about finding, developing and working with your inner resources i.e. allies that can support you in your PhD experience and beyond. With your allies to hand, you can be in a position of choice about what inner resources you need to bring to a situation. Here our question is what resources might you need to maintain, develop and support your authentic leader?

Challenge: Building up your allies

You already know your allies! You might though, especially in a more difficult moment of your PhD, have forgotten who they are and how they can help. So here's a way to playfully find them.

Find a relaxed space, with a piece of paper and coloured pens.

Imagine you are heading out on a journey in which are you are going to come across all kinds of adventures, from more peaceful moments of relaxation and reflection, to challenges your weren't expecting, to moments of real fun and laughter, moments that will require some thinking ahead, and moments where you will need so much creativity.

Choose the transport of your choice, be as creative as you like, the only constraint is that you need to take your allies with you: spaceship, hot air balloon, speed boat, an Atlantic cruiser, a bus, jeep, airplane, helicopter, canoe, bike, something else? The key thing is that whatever mode you choose, you need a team to help you drive it.

In charge of your transport and where you are heading is a leader. This leader can see the bigger picture clearly, they have a basic underlying wisdom. You might want to refer to this leader in different ways. It might be the captain, the director, the manager, the leader, the chief, the Guru, the guide, the authentic one, etc. Choose what you want to call this leader (you can be literal or choose something else like Charlie!).

As you head out on this adventure and come across different challenges, your leader needs different kinds of support. Who is available to come along? Who is going to join the team? Who are going to be the allies, available to call on when you need them?

Each of the following is a way to tap into some of these allies. You may not want all of these, and you may want more. With each, think back to a time when you experienced their character to really remember what it is like to have that resource:

- What would you call the ally who enables you to laugh?
- What would you call the ally who helps you plan ahead?
- What would you call the ally who wants to keep learning?
- What would you call the ally who knows how to find focus?
- What would you call the ally who says, 'time to chillax', to rest up?
- What would you call the ally who can make the right decisions?
- What would you call the ally who often has a hunch, has the intuition?
- What would you call the ally who really gets you going?
- What would you call the ally who keeps you balanced?

What other allies might you want to add here? The reflexive one? The doer? A gentle one? The healer?

For each of your allies, complete the following sentence:

My ally is called .... and her/his/its role is to ....

You can play with this: perhaps creating some sort of poster or even a picture of your 'vehicle' with the allies in it! That's up to you. The key thing here is to get to know them.

Examples of PhD allies

My ally is called *Bernard the Cat* and his role is to keep me curious, to ask questions, to keep me hungry for learning, whatever the situation there is always something to learn.

My ally is called *Mrs Oak* and her role is to be the strong adult, to help me see what I am responsible for, what I can change and what I can't.

My ally is called *Explorer* and her job is to look for the adventure in whatever I experience, to be excited about what is going to appear around the corner, to feel the fear and do it anyway.

My ally is called *Maggie Motivator* and it is her job to set the goals, keep me driven even when it feels tough.

My ally is called the *Giving Goat* and its job is to look for the contribution I am making, to ask what else I can give.

My ally is called *My Mate* and it is her job to check I'm looking after myself, keeping myself recharged.

My ally is called *Olly Organizer* and his job is to plan ahead, to make sure I know what to focus on when the time is right.

My ally is called *Mrs Doubtfire* and her job is to keep my confidence alive, to keep away the self-doubting Gremlins, and to make sure I approach things in the best way I can.

Getting to know your allies is one thing, choosing how you are going to use them to bring authenticity to your PhD experience and beyond is another! It's perhaps easier to notice what resources you have during the better times. If you think about those moments that are going well, where you feel your authenticity is in the flow, you can start to see those allies that you bring to the fore with apparent ease. What is perhaps a little harder is to spot how you might draw on those allies during those moments when authenticity feels harder to achieve.

Challenge: Getting your allies on board

Having learnt something about the allies you have chosen to have on board, the next task is learning how to awaken them and draw on them when you need to.

Think about PhD work you are facing this week. It might be a specific event (e.g. meeting with supervisors or a presentation), it might be an on-going piece of work (e.g. some analysis or writing or computer programming), it might be something you are stuck with (e.g. how to make sense of a theory, how to move forward with fieldwork), or something you are thinking about in the future (e.g. life after the PhD).

Remember, your leader is always there. Who does that leader need support from to bring authenticity to this work? Which allies need to step up to the game to help you be at your best? Do you need some allies that will help you get creative? To have fun? To feel confident? Organized? Driven? The doer? What combination of allies does your leader need to keep you moving in a way that realizes your authenticity?

Bringing out the authentic leader in you is not always straightforward and things move on. As the world around you changes and you learn more about yourself, what it means to be authentic and what it requires from you will change. You can be an authentic leader now even though what it means to be an authentic leader will change for you over time. The question we want to turn to now is, what changes have you experienced in you as a result of engaging with this book?

Write your own PhD experience story

Throughout this book we have presented short vignettes to illustrate some of the ways in which PhD students have changed their experience. Each vignette has drawn attention to what sometimes seem quite typical PhD experiences. While that may be true, the experience will always be unique to you and so too will the type of solution you find and the change that you experience. The vignettes have shown the difficulty the PhD student was facing, the learning process they went through, what they changed and the impact of that change. Each is there to provoke your curiosity and creativity in changing your PhD experience. The question is, then, in what ways have you changed your PhD experience for the better by engaging with this book?

In this way, we leave the last word to you.

Challenge: Write your own vignette

We want you to write your own vignette. We suggest you aim for between 300 and 500 words and here are some questions to prompt you:

- What were you experiencing when you began reading this book? What did you want to change?
- What provoked you to change your experience? What was the realization that enabled you to take a different perspective? What assumptions did you have to challenge?
- How did you make a change?
- What are you doing differently? And how is that helping you?
- Where are you now?

We'd love to hear your story. You can share your vignette, anonymously if you prefer, on our website 'yourphdcoach.com'.

References and further reading

Adrienne, C. (1998) *The Purpose of Your Life: Finding Your Place in the World Using Synchronicity, Intuition, and Uncommon Sense*. New York: Eagle Brook.

Buzan, T. (1984) *Make the Most of Your Mind*. New York: Linden.

Buzan, T. (2002) *How to Mind Map*. London: Thorsons.

Cameron, J. (1992) *The Artist's Way: A Spiritual Path to Higher Creativity*. Los Angeles, CA: Jeremy P. Tarcher/Perigee.

Carson, R.D. (2003) *Taming Your Gremlin: A Surprisingly Simple Method for Getting Out of Your Own Way*. New York: Quill.

Castaneda, C. (1990) *A Separate Reality*. New York: Simon & Schuster.

Covey, S.R. (1989) *The 7 Habits of Highly Effective People: Restoring the Character Ethic*. New York: Simon & Schuster.

Covey, S.R. (2004) *The 7 Habits of Highly Effective People: Powerful Lessons in Personal Change*, 2nd edn. New York: Simon & Schuster.

Crum, T.F. (1987) *The Magic of Conflict*. New York: Simon & Schuster.

Csikszentmihyayli, M. (1996) *Creativity: Flow and the Psychology of Discovery and Invention*. London: HarperCollins.

Csikszentmihyayli, M. (2002) *Flow: The Psychology of Happiness: The Classic Work on How to Achieve Happiness*, new edn. London: Rider.

Dills, R.B. (1991) *Tools for Dreamers: Strategies for Creativity and the Structure of Innovation*. Cupertino, CA: Meta Publications.

Frankl, V.E. (1963) *Man's Search for Meaning: An Introduction to Logotherapy*. New York: Simon & Schuster.

Gallwey, W.T. (1997) *The Inner Game of Tennis*, rev. edn. New York: Random House.

Gallwey, W.T., Hanzelik, E.S. and Horton, J. (2009) *The Inner Game of Stress: Outsmart Life's Challenges and Fulfill Your Potential*. New York: Random House.

Goleman, D. (1995) *Emotional Intelligence*. New York: Bantam.

Greene, M. (2008) *Mastering Your Inner Critic*. Chichester: Summersdale.

Hackman, J.R. (2011) *Collaborative Intelligence: Using Teams to Solve Hard Problems*. San Francisco, CA: Berrett-Koehler.

HH Dalai Lama and Cutler, H.C. (1998) *The Art of Happiness: A Handbook for Living*. London: Hodder and Stoughton.

Jeffers, S.J. (1987) *Feel the Fear and Do It Anyway*. San Diego, CA: Harcourt Brace Jovanovich.

Jeffers, S.J. (1996) *End the Struggle and Dance with Life: How to Build Yourself up When the World Gets You Down*. New York: St. Martin's Press.

Kabat-Zinn, J. (2004) *Wherever You Go, There You Are*. London: Piatkus

Kahneman, D. (2011) *Thinking, Fast and Slow*. New York: Farrar, Straus and Giroux.

Kimsey-House, H., Kimsey-House, K., Sandahl, P. and Whitworth, L. (2011) *Co-active Coaching: Changing Business, Transforming Lives*, 3rd edn. Boston, MA: Nicholas Brealey.

McDermott, I. and Jago, W. (2002) *The NLP Coach: A Comprehensive Guide to Personal Well-being and Professional Success*. London: Piatkus.

McDermott, I. and O'Connor, L. (1996) *NLP and Health: Using NLP to Enhance Your Health and Well Being*. London: Thorsons.

Nhat Hanh, T. (2004) *Peace Begins Here: Palestinians and Israelis Listening to Each Other*. Berkeley, CA: Parralex Press.

Peck, M.S. (1993) *The Road Less Travelled*. London: Rider.

Prior, R. and O'Connor, J. (2000) *NLP and Relationships: Simple Strategies to Make Your Relationships Work*. London: Thorsons.

Scott, S. (2002) *Fierce Conversations: Achieving Success in Work and in Life, One Conversation at a Time*. London: Piatkus.

Seligman, M. (2002) *Authentic Happiness: Using the New Positive Psychology to Realize Your Potential for Lasting Fulfillment*. New York: Free Press.

Sue, M.P. (2007) *Toxic People: Decontaminate Difficult People at Work Without Using Weapons or Duct Tape*. Hoboken, NJ: John Wiley & Sons.

Tolle, E. (2004) *The Power of Now: A Guide to Spiritual Enlightenment*. London: Hodder.

Whitmore, J. (2002) *Coaching for Performance: GROWing People, Performance and Purpose*. London: Nicholas Brealey.

Taking Coaching Further

Will and Jeff offer coaching to PhD students, researchers, academics staff as well as undergraduates.

One to one coaching

- *offers* personalised coaching to meet your particular needs and agenda. Available by face to face, telephone and Skype. Whether you are struggling, mulling along or wanting to achieve more, coaching is about unlocking your potential to enable you to achieve your goals. Coaching provokes you to find your own answers, it encourages, supports and challenges as you make important choices towards realising your aspirations.

"The coaching helped me to find a way forward when I was feeling overwhelmed, and enabled me to actually enjoy the last few months of my PhD!"

Peer-2-Peer Coaching Skills Programmes

- provides participants with core coaching skills and techniques to enable them to thrive in their research while developing skills for the future. The emphasis of the programme is in enabling participants to use coaching skills in relationship with their peers as well as self-coaching. This provides PhD students with a skill set that can enhance their own research performance, enhance what they gain from other training programmes, as well as enhance their employability.

"If I hadn't taken this programme I think I would be carrying on trying to squeeze more time and energy out of what there already is - and I suppose possibly then extending my PhD into infinity"

PhD Self-leadership workshops

- one-day interactive workshops that enable you to apply and develop self-leadership skills in you research. Through various coaching techniques that challenge you to live your values and tap into your inner resources, the workshop will help you shape your PhD experience and take responsibility for what you get out of it. You will come out of the workshop with some introductory coaching tools as well as a commitment to make the changes that you identify as important.

"I came out of the workshop feeling much more positive, less overwhelmed"

For further details visit
www.yourphdcoach.com
or email coaching@yourphdcoach.com

'Get Sorted!' is a programme of workshops and group coaching for undergraduates who want to get more from their university experience. Contact us for more information.

Jeff and Will each have private coaching practices and together they run coaching programmes for Graduates and small business leaders.